All the flowers of all the tomorrows are in the seeds of today.
– Native American proverb

©2022 Catherine Fet · North Landing Books · All Rights Reserved

POWHATAN
ruled Powhatan Confederacy 1545 – 1618

Wahunsenacah, better known as Chief Powhatan, was the head of the Powhatan Confederacy – the union of Algonquin Native American tribes in present-day Virginia. Chief Powhatan inherited from his mother the leadership of 6 tribes. He was a skillful diplomat, and – like most leaders of that era – he was ruthless when it came to political gain. He talked some chiefs of smaller tribes into joining his confederacy. Others he killed and replaced with his sons. In the end Powhatan ruled 30 tribes that paid him tribute for protection from the Iroquois – another powerful tribal union in eastern Virginia. Powhatan used war as a means of keeping his tribes united. He organized multi-tribe scalp hunts and raids to plunder native nations that were not part of the Powhatan confederacy.

In 1607, when the English established a colony in Jamestown, Virginia, Chief Powhatan was about 70 years old. He didn't believe the English were a threat. They settled on swampy badlands Powhatan tribes didn't care for. So Chief Powhatan didn't discourage contact with the colonists. The famous Captain John Smith wrote that the local tribal chiefs "kindly entertained" the colonists who visited them. The native people were "dancing, and offering strawberries, mulberries, bread, fish, and other country provisions." The colonists responded with their own gifts – "bells, pins, needles, and glass beads."

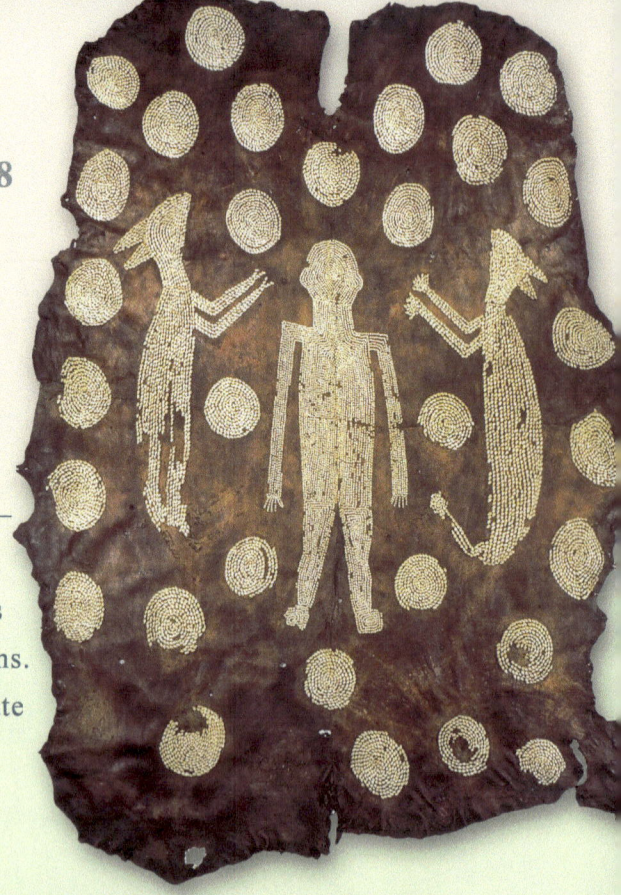

"Powhatan's Mantle" – a deer-hide hanging embroidered with roanoke (white shell beads). It may be one of the gifts sent by Powhatan to King James I.

MATRILINEAL SOCIETIES

Like most North American native tribes, the Powhatans were a matrilineal society, which means that kids were raised in the clans of their mothers, not those of their fathers. Families inherited their status and wealth only from their mothers' families. Often the elders, the members of the tribal council, and the chief were all chosen by women of the tribe.

SCALPING

Scalping was a practice of tearing a piece of skin, with hair attached, from the head of a dead enemy, to display as a trophy.

Captain John Smith

In 1607 John Smith was 28, a fast thinker, and a fearless adventurer. His military career began in France, in the service of Henry of Navarre. Later, fighting against the Turks in Hungary, he was taken prisoner, sold on a slave market, and sent to the Crimea. As a slave, with an iron collar on his neck, he was chained and regularly beaten. One day he freed himself, broke his master's skull with a flail, stole a horse, and fled. He ended up in Morocco where he joined the crew of an English warship. The Virginia colonists respected and feared John Smith. Chief Powhatan regarded Smith as a potential ally against the Iroquois.

Not all local tribes were friendly to the Jamestown colonists. Many were suspicious, because the newcomers behaved like they were going to stay on the Indian land forever. One day 200 native warriors attacked Jamestown fort. After an hour of fighting, the attackers were scared away by cannon fire and left. Eleven colonists were wounded and a boy killed. From that day on, such attacks continued.

Not long after the settlement was begun, Smith was ambushed by a group of Indian warriors led by Opechancanough, half-brother of Chief Powhatan. Seizing the Indian guide who had accompanied him, Smith used the guide as a shield against the arrows, while shooting with his pistol. However, soon he found himself surrounded by 200 native tribesmen. They stopped shooting, laid down their bows and demanded that he cast his pistol on the ground. Smith obeyed. "Having seized me, they led me to the king (Opechancanough)," wrote John Smith. "I gave him as a gift my compass, describing as well as I could how to use it. He was so amazed at it, that he allowed me to tell him about the roundness of the Earth, the course of the sun, moon, stars, and planets." The chief responded by treating Captain Smith to a meal. "I expected they would execute me," Smith recalled, "yet they treated me with what kindness they could. For supper I had a quarter of venison and some ten pounds of bread; what I left was reserved for me. Each morning three women brought me large platters of fine bread, and more venison than ten men could eat. My compass and tablets were returned to me."

Smith asked for permission to send word to his friends at Jamestown. He used a burnt stick to write a note on a piece of bark, and gave it to a messenger to take to the colony. The messenger delivered the note, and came back with presents. North American native tribes didn't have written languages. Smith's captors suspected that any man who could make a piece of bark talk by marking it with strange signs, was a magician. A few days after his capture, Smith was taken to Powhatan himself. Here is how he described his meeting with Powhatan: "Their emperor was proudly lying upon a bedstead a foot high, upon 10 or 12 mats. He wore many strings of large pearls around his neck, and was covered with a big blanket of raccoon fur. At his head sat a woman, at his feet another. On each side, sitting on a mat upon the ground, were his chief warriors, and behind them young women, each having a long string of white beads over their shoulders, their heads painted red. At my entrance before the king all the people gave a great shout. The Queen of Appomattuck was appointed to bring me water to wash my hands, and another brought a bunch of feathers instead of a towel to dry them."

Smith observed that the "majestical" appearance of Powhatan made him admire the great chief. When Powhatan asked Smith why the English landed on his shores, Smith did not admit that they had come to start a permanent settlement. He lied, saying that his crew had been defeated by the Spanish, and the bad weather forced them to come ashore at Jamestown. "Powhatan kindly welcomed me with good words and large platters of various treats," wrote Smith, "assuring me of his friendship, and promising me liberty within 4 days. He promised to give me corn, venison, or whatever food I wanted (to take home for the colonists). In return he wanted iron hatchets and copper." Satisfied with the agreement, Powhatan sent Captain Smith home to Jamestown.

This account of Smith's captivity was published in London soon after it was written. It did not mention Powhatan's daughter Pocahontas. So what is the origin of the romantic story about Pocahontas saving Captain Smith's life?

"Capture of Captain John Smith" by Elmer Boyd Smith

IRON

Native American tribes north of Rio Grande didn't have the technology of mining ore, smelting, and alloying metal. So they didn't have iron. Their tools and weapons were made from stone, animal horns, and bones. However, copper-bearing rocks could be found lying on the ground across North America. Native tribes cold-hammered copper into artistic or decorative objects, but it was too soft for making tools.

The story of Pocahontas only appeared in print much later, after Captain Smith told it in a letter to Queen Anne, the wife of King James I of England, in 1616. Very likely it was pure fiction. Here it is: "Two great stones were brought before Powhatan. They dragged Smith to the stones, and laid his head on them, ready to crush his skull with their clubs. Then Pocahontas, the king's dearest daughter, held his head in her arms and laid her own head upon his to save him from death. Seeing this, the emperor ordered that Smith should live to make him hatchets, and to provide his daughter bells and beads."

"Pocahontas" by Elmer Boyd Smith

Modern historians believe that Powhatan didn't intend to kill Captain Smith. In many Native American tribes orphaned children and prisoners of war were adopted into Indian families through a special death and rebirth ritual. The ritual imitated the death of the person to be adopted and their rebirth into a new family. It's likely that John Smith witnessed such a ceremony and misinterpreted it.

Peace with Powhatan was vital for Jamestown. The year the Jamestown colonists arrived in the New World, a crippling drought struck the Atlantic coast. The colonists had hardly any supplies and few good leaders. Most of them had been hired by the Virginia Company, not for their survival skills or leadership abilities, but for their service in Europe's religious wars. They had chosen a small peninsula in the swampy area up the James River because it was easy to defend. But there was no clean water or land suitable for farming in the area. Jamestown soon grew hungry and desperate.

Many of the Jamestown settlers were failed merchants, adventurers, and 'gentlemen' who had wasted their family fortunes. They expected to find gold and refused to work in the colony. They would rather plunder the Indian villages. "We didn't come here to work," they told Smith. "Then you shall not eat," he responded. Smith prohibited theft from Indian villages and insisted that the colonists behave with dignity. He even ran a daily log of swear words they used! At night a can of cold water was poured down the offenders' sleeves for each instance of swearing.

The following year John Smith, Captain Newport, and 20 other colonists from Jamestown went to Powhatan's village to barter European goods for food. They were met by 300 warriors who took them to Powhatan. Before Powhatan's house the Indians set out 50 large platters of bread. In his house Powhatan, dressed in a robe of fur, sat on a bed of reed mats, his leather pillow embroidered with pearls and white beads. He invited Smith to sit next to him and accepted Smith's gifts – a suit of red cloth, a white greyhound dog, and a hat. Captain Newport brought for Powhatan a 13-year-old English boy, who was supposed to remain with the Indians and learn to be an interpreter. In return, Powhatan gave Newport a bag of beans, and one of his tribesmen as a servant. Smith wrote about Powhatan, "he carried himself so proudly, yet discreetly, that he made us all admire his natural gifts."

A skilled negotiator, Powhattan told Newport, 'It is not agreeable with my greatness to bargain and trade for each small item. Therefore lay down all your goods at once. What I like I will take, and will give you what I think they are worth.'" Smith had warned Newport to offer one object at a time for barter. Native tribes came to value European goods, but the colonists had a limited supply of items from Europe, so they tried to barter as much food for the colony as they could for each object. Newport, however, was annoyed with Smith and laid out all the goods he had brought before Powhatan. Powhatan took every single item giving Newport only a few bushels of corn as payment. Newport expected to receive much more. He was devastated. But Smith, who was as skilled at bargaining as Powhatan, let Powhatan see, as if accidentally, a few blue beads which he pretended he did not wish to part with. They were of great price, he said, being the color of the sky. Such beads could be worn only by great kings. Now Powhatan had to have those beads! Smith let him have them, but charged Powhatan 300 bushels of corn.

CORN

Corn, or maize, comes from a wild grass (Teosinte) that was first cultivated in the South of Mexico about 7,000 years ago. A few hundred years before the arrival of Europeans in the Americas, corn was adopted by the North American native tribes. European trade spread it all over the world, along with other indigenous American plants, such as beans, squash, melons, and tobacco. For native people corn was one of the Three Sisters – corn, beans, and squash – grown together in the same patch. Corn stalks offered support for bean plants.

All went well until the Virginia Company that financed the Jamestown colony, ordered Smith and Newport to crown Chief Powhatan an English prince – to make him an oficial subject of the English king. John Smith objected to the crowning. Indeed, the ceremony ended up being awkward and meaningless. Here is how John Smith described it:

"The Coronation of Powhatan" by John Gadsby Chapman

"The presents were brought to Powhattan, a bed and furniture set up for him, a scarlet cloak and clothes put on him. But what trouble it was to make him kneel to receive his crown! He didn't know about the majesty or meaning of a crown, or the ceremony of the bending of the knee... At last, by pushing hard on his shoulders, he was made to stoop a little, and we put the crown on his head." The ship Discovery saluted with cannon fire, only to terrify the native people. Finally seeing that all was quiet, Powhatan "gave his old shoes and his mantle to Captain Newport" to thank him for the crown.

Told by their leaders that Powhatan was now the subject of the English king, Jamestown settlers expected the Powhatan tribes to provide them with food. Jamestown grew to 500 colonists and started expanding its territory toward the native villages. Meanwhile the native tribes were no longer willing to barter their corn for a little copper or a handful of beads. Powhatan asked Smith to send him workers who could build him a European-style house – with doors, windows and a fireplace, like the houses he saw in Jamestown. Smith sent some men to begin the work, and soon followed with others. On their way to Powhatan's town Smith and his companions stopped for a night with another friendly chief who warned them to beware of Powhatan: "Don't trust him. And be sure he has no chance to seize your arms. For he has sent for you only to cut your throats." In spite of this warning Smith traveled to see Powhatan. But when he asked Powhatan to barter for food, Powhatan said that in exchange for corn he would only accept guns or swords. "If you have forty swords I might find forty baskets of corn in exchange for them." Smith refused to supply Powhatan with weapons.

According to Smith, Powhatan also tried to convince the colonists to lay down their arms: "My people fear to bring you corn seeing you are all armed." Smith refused again, saying, "When your people come to Jamestown, we receive them with their bows and arrows. With you it must be the same." Of course, the only accounts of these exchanges between the native tribesmen and the colonists came from the colonists. Were they truthful? We'll never know. Desperate to provide food for the colony, Smith marched around with a drawn sword and loaded gun in his hands. He hinted that he would use force if Powhatan Indians refused to barter with Jamestown on his terms. The Indians loaded Smith's boats with corn. The relationship between Chief Powhatan and John Smith was destroyed.

That night, according to Smith, Powhatan decided to murder Smith and his companions, but Pocahontas secretly came to Smith's camp and told him about the possible attack. To show his gratitude, Smith offered her "anything she delighted in, but with the tears rolling down her cheeks she said she dared not take anything, for if Powhatan found out, she would be dead. And she ran away alone, as she came."

"Pocahontas warns Captain Smith of danger" by Elmer Boyd Smith

Next, a few native men arrived at the colonists' cabin, each carrying a basket of hot food that smelled delicious. They asked the Englishmen to lay aside their arms and sit down to supper. But Captain Smith would take no chances. Loaded gun in hand, he forced the messengers to taste each dish, to be certain that none of them was poisoned. Smith stayed on guard all night. At dawn the colonists left.

In October 1609 Smith was injured in a gunpowder explosion and left for England. Powhatan was told that Smith was dead. With Smith gone, the Jamestown colonists grew even lazier. They mistreated native people constantly. Enraged by their behavior, Chief Powhatan ordered his warriors to kill any colonists who left the Jamestown fort. This period is known as the Starving Time. Having run out of food the settlers ate rats, dogs, horses, and even corpses. 80% of them died of disease and starvation. In May 1610, a supply ship arrived in Jamestown bringing a new governor, Thomas Gates. Finding only 60 settlers alive, he ordered everyone to return to England. But then another ship came, bringing English nobleman Thomas West. West took control of the colony and started a policy of 'no compromise' toward the Powhatan tribes. Clashes between the colonists and the Powhatan warriors led to the First Powhatan War. Many Jamestown settlers perished, and two smaller local tribes were nearly destroyed.

In 1613 West left for England. Samuel Argall, the new Jamestown governor, captured Pocahontas, and that made Powhatan reach out to the colonists for peace. Powhatan died in 1618, having never again resumed a friendly relationship with the English.

"The Young Chief Uncas" by John Mix Stanley; vintage magazines; Shawnee mocassins (1810)

POCAHONTAS
1596 – 1617

Pocahontas' birth name was Amonute – 'a gift' – but she later took another name, Matoaka – 'flower between two streams.' 'Pocahontas' was her childhood nickname. Its meaning is 'a playful one.'

Many books and films tell the romantic story of Pocahontas falling in love with Captain John Smith, and saving his life. Is it a true story? Unlikely. Captain Smith came up with the 'saving his life' story when Pocahontas became famous in England, years after he left Jamestown. There was never any indication of any personal relationship between John Smith and Pocahontas before that. The story of their love is just that – a story.

Once John Smith started trading with the Powhatan tribes, 10-year-old Pocahontas, accompanied by Powhatan warriors, was sent by her father to Jamestown, to ask for the release of some tribesmen held prisoner at the fort. She brought a deer and bread for the colonists. Captain Smith gave Pocahontas a few small gifts, freed the prisoners "in regard to her father's kindness," and asked Pocahontas to tell her dad how well the captives had been treated.

From that moment on, Pocahontas began coming to Jamestown with Powhatan tribesmen who delivered food to the colony.

NATIVE AMERICAN BREAD

Native American tribes baked cornbread. They also made bread from bean flour and from oak-tree acorn flour. They added salt and honey to the dough.

The official portrait of Pocahontas created during her visit to London and "Pocahontas" by Jean Leon Gerome Ferris

She played with Jamestown kids, teaching them how to do cartwheels, how to play a native ball game, and telling them about life in native villages. In exchange, colonists explained European manners and customs, and told Pocahontas about their Christian faith.

LACROSSE

Lacrosse comes from a native ball game played by North American native tribes of the eastern Woodlands.

"Ball Play of the Choctaw" and "A Ball Player" by George Catlin

But when Captain Smith left for England (never to return), conflicts between the English and the Powhatan Indians grew into the First Powhatan War. Powhatan tribes retreated deeper inland, and Pocahontas stopped coming to Jamestown. When Captain Samuell Argall took the secufrity of Jamestown into his hands, he decided to kidnap Pocahontas so that she could be exchanged for some English prisoners, tools, and guns that had been seized by Powhatan tribesmen. Hearing that Pocahontas was nearby, in the Patawomeck village, Argall bribed the village chief with a copper kettle, and asked him to lure Pocahontas on board his ship. To get Pocahontas back, Chief Powhatan freed the English prisoners, but he couldn't find all the weapons and tools he was supposed to return to Jamestown, so Captain Argall did not free Pocahontas. He held her for almost a year in the English settlement of Henricus, north of Jamestown.

In Henricus Pocahontas was treated well. A local minister taught her English and studied the Bible with her. She also met John Rolfe, a Virginia tobacco farmer and her future husband.

"The Kidnapping of Pocahontas" by Jean Leon Gerome Ferris

John Rolfe started a tobacco plantation, Varina Farms. He was a widower. His wife and daughter perished in a shipwreck on their way to Virginia. While a prisoner, Pocahontas taught John Rolfe how to grow sweet tobacco.

TOBACCO

Despite continuing clashes between the colonists and the Powhatan Indians, at some point the English allowed Pocahontas to see her father, Chief Powhatan. Reportedly, she told her dad that he valued her "less than old swords and axes" and told him she would stay

Tobacco had been cultivated by native American tribes since at least 1000 BC. Europeans first saw native people smoke tobacco leaves during Columbus' voyages. By the end of the 16th century tobacco smoking became popular in Europe. Jamestown colonists found tobacco so profitable that they planted it even in the streets of their fort, and used tobacco leaves as money.

with the colonists "who loved her." It's likely that she and John Rolfe had already decided to get married, because soon Rolfe wrote a letter to the acting governor, Thomas Dale, telling him that he had been in love with Pocahontas for a long time and would like to propose her marriage.

When Dale learned that Pocahontas agreed to become a Christian and marry John Rolfe, he canceled the prisoner exchange that involved Pocahontas. He knew that the first marriage between an Englishman and a native woman would capture the imagination of the public in England, and allow the Virginia Company to raise more money for Jamestown.

In 1614 Pocahontas was baptized and took the Christian name Rebecca. Powhatan was invited to his daughter's wedding. This ended the First Powhatan War. The 'Peace of Pocahontas' lasted 8 years. When King James I heard about the marriage, he was angry: Now that Rolfe is married to the Indian princess, what if he joined forces with the Indians and took over Virginia? But Rolfe was not interested in politics. For two years he and Pocahontas lived at Varina Farms, where their son, Thomas, was born.

"Marriage of Pocahontas" by Henry Brueckner

In 1616, in order to generate financial support for Jamestown, the Virginia Company invited the Rolfe family to visit London. On the trip they were accompanied by representatives of Chief Powhatan, including the medicine man (a native priest) Tomocomo – whom Powhatan had ordered to count all the people in England!

In England Pocahontas became an instant celebrity. She was presented as 'Lady Rebecca' at court where she met King James and Queen Anne. Courtiers addressed Pocahontas as 'Princess,' remained standing before her, and walked backwards when they left her presence. The Queen took Pocahontas to theaters and concerts. London aristocrats competed in holding dinners and receptions in her honor. Poets composed songs about her. Pocahontas had her official portrait painted and an engraving portrait was also made to commemorate her visit. An inn was named after her – in French – 'La Belle Sauvage' ('The Beautiful Savage').

While she was in London, Captain Smith came to see her. Pocahontas was disappointed that Smith didn't treat her as an old friend, but as a princess. She was also angry at the Jamestown colonists who had told her Captain Smith was dead.

THE MEDICINE MAN

Among the native tribes of North America, a medicine man (or medicine woman) is a healer and spiritual leader, similar to a priest. The medicine man is also the keeper of tribal traditions and knowledge. The term 'medicine man' is of European origin, and refers to only the healing aspect of this work.

NATIVE COUNTING SYSTEMS

North American native societies used various counting systems. Since they didn't have writing, they recorded numbers by making notches in wood, knots on strings, or woven pieces of art. Most counting was done on fingers. Some tribes had an understanding of multiplication, and could count up to 1000 using their fingers.

When the Rolfes were leaving for Virginia, on the trip down the Thames River, Pocahontas and her son Thomas became ill, and Pocahontas died. John Rolfe returned to Virginia alone, leaving Thomas in England with his brother.

The native priest Tomocomo didn't like what he saw in England. The English could not be trusted, he concluded. His report to Chief Powhatan was so negative that it probably contributed to the ever growing tensions between the colonists and the native tribes.

John Rolfe died in 1622 – most likely in The Indian Massacre – a deadly raid in which Powhatan Indians killed over 300 colonists. The raid was organized by Pocahontas' uncle, Opechancanough, who took over the Powhatan Confederacy in 1618, after Chief Powhatan's death.

"The Baptism of Pocahontas"
by John Gadsby Chapman

OPECHANCANOUGH
1554 – 1646

By the time Opechancanough became chief of the Powhatan Confederacy, the patience of Powhatan Indians with the English colonists was coming to an end. The colonists felt they were entitled to the land they had discovered, because, from their point of view, most of it was uninhabited. So, as they started growing tobacco, they kept expanding their plantations onto the land of the Powhatan tribes. No longer dependent on bartering with the native people, the English settlers did not even try to be nice. Clashes with the Indians became common.

There were colonists who believed that peace with the Indians was impossible as long as the English treated the native people as 'wild savages' 'out there'. They tried to correct the wrongs. For example, the Virginia House of Burgesses, established in 1619, defended local tribesmen against one of the plantation owners. But in 1621, Opechancanough's war chief, Nemattanew, supposedly killed one of the settlers and stole his clothes. In response the settlers attacked and killed Nemattanew. It's likely that this moved Opechancanough to finally make up his mind to destroy Jamestown in the event known as The Indian Massacre of 1622.

Opechancanough and his brother took 'war names,' and went from tribe to tribe calling on the native people to unify in order to drive the English off their land once and for all. However, Opechanacanough was careful to conceal his plan. When Nemattanew was killed, he pretended to agree that Nemattanew had been punished justly. To obtain the colonists' trust, Opechancanough's warriors went to them asking to be taught about Christianity and to be baptized. Even Opechancanough got baptized. The English became convinced that the Powhatan tribes were reaching out for peace. Meanwhile the Powhatan natives who traded with the colonists were gathering intelligence on how many people were in various settlements, and at what times of day they were in the fields.

NATIVE LAND OWNERSHIP

Most native tribes of North America were nomadic or semi-nomadic. Colonists saw them move from place to place, and concluded that the land didn't belong to anyone. Actually, native tribes had a very clear idea which hunting grounds, trails, or fishing areas belonged to each tribe. But there was no individual land ownership, no system of laws protecting ownership, and no permanent buildings or regularly cultivated fields that would point to who owned the land.

On the morning of March 22, 1622, Powhatan tribesmen came to a number of English settlements and tobacco plantations bringing deer, turkeys, fish, or fruit for sale. Others borrowed the boats of the settlers to cross the rivers and visit the outlying plantations. But at noon, in an instant, the scene changed from peace to terror. Knives and tomahawks were drawn and the native warriors started slaughtering the settlers – all of them, men, women, and children alike. To terrify the English even more, they mutilated the bodies of the dead.

Opchanacanough's plan was to drive the colonists away by fear, not by weapons. Whenever the colonists happened to be armed and opposed the native warriors, the Powhatans fled without fighting. Next, Powhatan warriors headed for Jamestown, but a native boy who had converted to Christianity warned his English friend of the conspiracy, and the Jamestown settlers had time to bar the gates. Powhatan tribesmen circled around the fort threatening the settlers, but soon left. The farmers who had survived the attack were ordered to abandon their fields and shelter in Jamestown. Some settlers refused to obey the order, arming their servants and bringing cannons to defend their homes. Nevertheless, of the 80 English farms only 6 remained.

Opechancanough refuses to negotiate with Sir Francis Wyatt, colonial Governor of Virginia

The number of the settlers killed in the massacre is usually given as 347. Over 700 more died of starvation the next year, because of the destruction of the farms. Opechancanough could have continued the attack, but he fully relied on the fear factor, believing that the colonists would simply leave. Instead, the English started rebuilding their farms, and the Virginia Company sent over 1000 new colonists to Jamestown.

Then the survivors of the massacre began burning Indian villages for revenge. Whenever Powhatan tribesmen showed up close to Jamestown, they were shot down. If they escaped, the farmers chased them with bloodhounds into the forest, and had the dogs kill them. Whenever a white man was within reach of the Powhatan warriors, he was slaughtered on the spot or dragged off to die by torture. The Second Powhatan War had begun.

While the Europeans fought wars by marching in formation and attacking the enemy in an open field, Indian warfare was guerilla style: Powhatan warriors attacked settlers in small groups and then disappeared into woodlands. Unable to scare them far enough away from Jamestown, the colonists decided to give Opechancanough the taste of his own medicine and win by deception.

They asked to meet with the Powhatan chiefs to negotiate a peace treaty. When the chiefs arrived they were offered poisoned wine. Once the poisoned chiefs were dead, the colonists slaughtered over 200 warriors that came as part of the Powhatan delegation, and burned down the villages of the local tribes. Three years later, in 1626, Opechancanough asked for peace.

ROACH HEADDRESS

Roach is a traditional male headdress of the New England Native American tribes made from porcupine, moose, or deer hair, and dyed in bright colors. Below: 19th-century Roach headdress from the Eastern Plains

The peace didn't last long. Opechancanough saw the English plantations spreading ever more widely. Tobacco became so profitable, that the plantation owners started bringing Africans as slaves to work in the fields. More and more slaves were arriving, and the tobacco farmers kept seizing the Powhatan hunting grounds without regard for the agreements and rights of the native tribes. The numbers of white and African inhabitants of Virginia outgrew the numbers of Powhatan Indians. The English built a palisade – a 6-mile-long stockade wall stretching across the Virginia Peninsula, to keep the Powhatans away.

In 1643, 21 years after the Indian Massacre, Opechancanough decided to make one last attempt to get rid of Jamestown. He was now over 90 years old, but his authority over his tribes was as strong as ever. He summoned every single Powhatan warrior and led them to break through the palisade wall and raid the English settlements. In this surprise attack between 400 and 500 colonists were killed. This was the beginning of The Third Powhatan War.

Soon Governor William Berkeley, with a force of armed colonists, was again raiding Powhatan lands, this time looking for Opchanacanough. Most of the Powhatan warriors were killed in these attacks. Their families were sold into slavery. Eventually, Opchanacanough was captured, and brought to Jamestown in chains.

Berkeley wanted to send Opchanacanough to England as a royal captive, where he would be held in custody until his death. While waiting to be taken to England, Opchanacanough was placed in a cage in the middle of Jamestown. As the crowd gathered around to look at him, Opechancanough asked to see the governor, and when William Berkeley arrived, the chief said, "Had it been my fortune to have taken you prisoner, I would not have exposed you as a show to my people."

One of the colonists, who was guarding Opchanacanough's cage, was a survivor of a Powhatan raid. Resentful that Berkeley spared Opchanacanough's life, he disobeyed orders and shot Opchanacanough in the back, killing him.

"Hunters" by John Mix Stanley

"Indian captives" by Robert Walter Weir

After Opchanacanough's death, the new Powhatan chief was forced to sign a treaty that dissolved the Powhatan Confederacy and confined surviving native people to reservations — small areas of their ancestral lands to which they had rights as long as they lived in peace with the colonists.

Samoset & Massasoit
1590 – 1653   1581 – 1661

In November 1620, the famous ship The Mayflower, carrying the Pilgrims, arrived at the coast of modern-day Massachusetts. The Pilgrims started building log cabins and trying to provide food for their colony. Their relationship with the native people there started in a disaster. One day, hungry and desperate, the Pilgrims stole some corn buried by the local Nauset tribespeople in the sand. They said they had taken only a small part of the corn stash in order to plant it in spring, and that they were planning to pay for it, but, from the standpoint of the native tribe, it was theft. In response, the Nauset warriors attacked the Pilgrims. Mayflower captain Miles Standish shot the ship's cannon to scare away the attackers, and, fortunately, no one on either side was injured.

Weeks passed. Day by day the stock of provisions brought from England grew smaller. The settlers were put on such small rations that sometimes they had only six grains of wheat for a meal. The Pilgrims were not good hunters or experienced fishermen. They survived almost entirely on shellfish. As a result, between December and March half of the Plymouth settlers died of disease and malnutrition.

The local tribes remained a threat. Concerned about the colony's safety, Standish called a meeting to discuss building a fort. As they gathered in the common house, suddenly a native man walked in – a tall warrior, whose deerskin clothes were trimmed in fur. Three eagle feathers were braided into his long black hair. Lines of red and black were painted on his face. He carried a bow, and a quiver of arrows.

*Left: "Pilgrims Landing"
by Peter Rothermel
Above: "Mayflower in Plymouth Harbor"
by William Halsall*

The Pilgrims sprang to their feet and drew their guns and swords, but the Indian did not move. In silence, he looked at the settlers solemnly and said, "Welcome, Englishmen!" He pulled two arrows from his quiver – one with a stone arrowhead, and one without. These were symbols of war and peace.

The name of the unexpected visitor was Samoset. He was the chief of the Eastern Abenaki Native American tribe. This area was ruled by the Wampanoag tribal confederacy (a union of tribes under the Wampanoag leadership), so Samoset was either visiting the Wampanoag chief, Massasoit, or was his prisoner. Samoset had picked up some English from sailors on ships that had been sent to explore the North American coast. He knew their captains by name and referred to them as friends. That's why Massasoit had chosen Samoset to make the first contact with the Plymouth settlers.

The Pilgrims asked Samoset to sit with them in the common house. Samoset suggested that Indians could bring furs to trade. He also told the Pilgrims about a local tribesman named Squanto who spoke really good English and could be an interpreter.

Samoset was curious to see the village of the Puritans, so they gave him a tour. He walked around marveling at the doors and windows of their cottages. When night came he was still in the village. One of the colonists, Stephen Hopkins, invited Samoset to stay at his house for the night. Hopkins had previously lived at Jamestown in Virginia, where he learned some Algonquian language from the Powhatans. Samoset spoke Algonquian, so they could talk to each other. Then Samoset spread a deerskin on the floor and fell asleep before the fireplace. In the morning the Pilgrims gave him gifts – a knife, a bracelet, and a ring – and invited the Wampanoag tribe to trade in furs, as Samoset had suggested.

Two days later Samoset came back with five native tribesmen. They wore deerskin clothes, their hair was decorated with long eagle feathers and fox tails, and each man carried a roll of fine furs. In exchange for the furs the Indians wanted objects made of metal – bowls, kettles, and knives. Knives were especially valuable to them.

NATIVE CROP PATCHES

Since North American native tribes had no metal, they plowed the earth using animal horns and sticks. Their stone axes were not sharp enough to cut down trees. Instead they burned the tree bark, so that the tree died and the sun would shine through the naked branches on the corn patch. Metal blades brought by Europeans were used to plant and harvest crops, among many other uses. The Indian tribes usually moved their crop patches to a new area every 5-10 years to avoid overusing the land.
<< A 'three sisters' patch in Arizona

The Pilgrims treated their guests to dinner. After the meal the six Indians danced and sang in a ritual that looked both beautiful and mysterious. A few days later native tribesmen were spotted near the Plymouth colony. Captain Standish and another colonist, Edward Winslow, went forward to meet them. "This is Squanto, friend of the English," said Samoset. "We are here because Massasoit, our Chief, wants to meet your Chief."

Massasoit, the Great Sachem (Chief) of the Wampanoag, was uncertain what to do about the newcomers. Plymouth colony was the first settlement in his area. Europeans that had visited before stayed on their ships and left quickly. At first Massasoit had hoped to drive the Pilgrims away by holding ritual gatherings where his chief medicine men called on the spirits of the land to destroy the settlement. But the Pilgrims had survived.

Meanwhile, the contact between the native tribes and the Europeans resulted in the exchange of infectious diseases. Native Americans had no immunity against diseases that originated in Europe. Such a large number of Wampanoag Indians were dying from them, that the weakened Massasoit's confederacy was forced to pay tribute to the powerful Narragansett tribe who lived deeper inland. Now Massasoit felt that the Plymouth colonists could be his allies against the Narragansett.

POW-WOW

The word "pow-wow" comes from the Narragansett language and means "a spiritual leader." Native people across North America had a variety of public rituals, such as dances and competitions dedicated to spirits, war- or peace-making gatherings, and healing ceremonies. In the 19th century Americans started using the word "pow-wow" to describe any events bringing together native people for traditional rituals or celebrations. Today pow-wows are festivals of Native American culture and tradition.

Samoset and Squanto invited the Pilgrim leader, Governor Carver, to come with them to the Wampanoag camp, but Carver refused, fearing a trap. They finally decided that Chief Massasoit would come to the Plymouth colony, while Edward Winslow would stay at the Indian camp as a hostage.

When Winslow met Massasoit, he was impressed at the kingly appearance of the chief. Massasoit's deerskin clothes were beautifully trimmed with shells and quills, and he wore a crown of eagle feathers that streamed down over his shoulders and all the way to the ground. His face was covered with red mineral paint, and he had a little bag of tobacco on a chain of white bone beads worn around his neck. Winslow spread a red blanket on the grass, and placed on it the gifts for Massasoit – strings of beads, knives, and a long copper chain. "My chief sends you these gifts and invites you to his house. He wants to be your friend," said Winslow. With 20 of his warriors, Massasoit went to the colony, led by Squanto. Captain Standish and a few settlers, dressed in their best clothes and armor, met Massasoit and his men and took them to the common house, where a large rug was spread and cushions were laid for the chief and his warriors. The sound of a trumpet and drums announced the arrival of Governor Carver.

QUILLWORK

Native people of North America used porcupine quills to decorate their clothes. Quills were dyed and stitched to deerskin using animal sinews.

Above: Massasoit and Governor Carver smoke the Peace Pipe

Right: Tobacco bag decorated with quillwork, 1870

Right: Massasoit visits Plymouth colony.

Food and drink were brought, and, after they ate, Governor Carver and Massasoit smoked the pipe of peace and made a treaty. Massasoit promised that his tribe would not harm the settlers, and, if other Indian tribes made war on Plymouth, Massasoit would protect the Pilgrims. Massasoit also promised that his tribesmen would not bring their bows and arrows into the colony. Governor Carver promised that the white men would not carry their guns into the Indian villages and that they would always pay a fair price for furs. Massasoit unrolled the gifts he had brought for the Plymouth governor – fine furs, a bow and arrows like his own, and a necklace of bear teeth. This treaty of peace between the Pilgrims and the Indians was kept for 50 years.

Soon after Massasoit made the treaty of friendship with the Plymouth colony, settlers Edward Winslow and Stephen Hopkins visited the sachem at his home. They reported that despite Massasoit's great power, his house was small, with only one bed made of wooden planks raised a foot off the ground. "The chief and his wife occupied one end of the bed," wrote Winslow, "and we slept on the other." Two of Massasoit's bodyguards slept right next to the guests.

One day word came to the Pilgrims that Massasoit was sick and dying. Edward Winslow packed a small bottle of medicine and some food, and rushed to Massasoit's village. The door of Massasoit's house was a curtain of fine fur. Inside, next to Massasoit's bed, Winslow saw a few medicine men who were chanting, stomping, leaping, and waving their arms in order to drive away the evil spirits who – they believed – made the chief sick. Massasoit had a high fever and his throat was so sore he could hardly swallow. He had eaten nothing for days. Winslow opened his basket and realized that the bottle of medicine he had brought with him was broken. There was not a drop left. He looked around the house, and, finding some corn, edible roots, and strawberry leaves, he improvised a soup.

WETU

The typical house of the Wampanoag was called a wetu. It was made from wooden poles bent into arches. The roof was covered with bark and woven mats. Most North American native tribes led a partially nomadic life. When the tribe decided to move, they would dismantle their home, and travel, carrying - on their shoulders - the poles that supported the roof and the materials used to make the walls – bark, animal skins, and woven mats. Owning large houses was not viewed as practical or prestigious.

Wetu, 1897

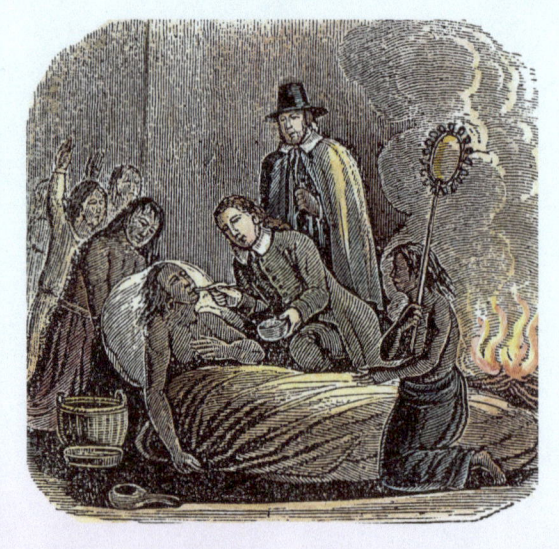

He fed Massasoit and asked the medicine men to leave so Massasoit could fall asleep. Food and sleep worked. In two or three days, Massasoit recovered, and Indian families started coming from miles and miles around to see Winslow, the now-famous 'medicine man.'

Everything we know about Samoset and Massasoit comes from two memoirs of the Mayflower Pilgrims – *Of Plymouth Plantation* by Governor William Bradford and *Mourt's Relation*, written by William Bradford and Edward Winslow.

"A hunter" and *"An Indian canoe"* by Herbert Herget
Below: *"A weaver"* by Robert Wesley Amick
and *"A Black Foot medicine man"* vintage print

SQUANTO
1585 – 1622

Squanto belonged to the Native American Patuxet tribe, one of the bands of the Wampanoag tribal confederation. His real name was Tisquantum. Squanto was a nickname given to him by Europeans. In 1614, Squanto and 23 other Indians were kidnapped by the English fishing boat captain Thomas Hunt, who took them to Spain hoping to sell them to Muslim slave traders. But when Hunt came ashore in Malaga and tried to sell his captives, he was confronted by the local Catholic friars (monks) who condemned slavery. The friars forced him to free his captives. The monks took Squanto and the others to their monastery. But Squanto didn't like it at the monastery, and, leaving Spain, he made it to England where he found work with shipbuilders. While in England, Squanto met Captain John Smith and maybe even Pocahontas who was in London at that very time!

In 1619 Captain Thomas Dermer hired Squanto as an interpreter for an expedition to Newfoundland. In Newfoundland, Squanto convinced the captain to sail down the coast to New England – to trade with Squanto's tribe! But when they arrived at his native village near present-day Cape Cod, he discovered that his tribe had been wiped out by smallpox. The Indians of Nauset and Massachusetts, who remembered the kidnapping by Hunt, attacked Captain Dermer's crew. Dermer was wounded and soon died, and Squanto was probably taken prisoner and sent to Massasoit.

In 1621 Samoset brought Squanto to the Plymouth colony, and Massasoit told him to remain at Plymouth and help the settlers as much as he could. The Pilgrims were glad to have Squanto with them. He helped them in many ways. They did not know how to plant corn. It was Squanto who taught them. By watching the trees, native people knew the perfect planting time. "See, oak leaves are as big as a squirrel's ear," Squanto said. "Time to plant corn now." Squanto taught the settlers to use fish as fertilizer for corn. From him the Pilgrims learned how to cook corn, and make ropes, shoes and mats out of corn husks. They also twisted and wove husks to make seats for their chairs. Squanto knew every path in the forest, he knew where the deer went to drink, and in which streams to find beavers. He taught colonists to make snares of willow twigs to catch fish, and how to build bear traps from logs. He made a whistle out of reeds that sounded like the cry of a turkey or a wild duck, and lured the birds toward the hunters. Squanto could go through the forest without breaking a twig. He could move through the tall grass without being seen.

Edward Winslow asked Squanto to teach him the language of the local tribes and soon they switched from English to Algonquian. In return Squanto wanted to learn to read. He always

"The first Thanksgiving" by Jean Leon Gerome Ferris

marveled at books – the 'talking leaves.' The only book Winslow had in his house was the Bible. It was the book from which he had learned to read, so he used it to teach Squanto reading.

Pilgrims worked in their fields from morning till night preparing for the next long winter, and finally the harvest was done. "Friends," said Governor Bradford, "God has blessed our summer's work, and sent us a bountiful harvest. Let's set aside time to celebrate and give thanks to God. What say you? Shall we not have a week of feasting and of thanksgiving?"

Early the next morning Squanto was sent to invite Massasoit to join the Pilgrims for a feast the following Thursday. This, as legend has it, was how the holiday of Thanksgiving came to be. Modern historians say there were Thanksgiving celebrations in other colonies as well, but we know for sure that the Pilgrims treated Massasoit to a feast. As Bradford and Edward Winslow write in their memoir, **Mourt's Relation**, "many of the Indians came to us, and among them their greatest king, Massasoit, with some 90 men, whom for three days we entertained and feasted." Massasoit and his warriors came to the Pilgrims' feast dressed in their finest clothes, wearing holiday paint and feathers. They all sat down at long tables. The women passed bowls of clam broth to each guest. There were piles of brown bread and sweet cakes, dishes of turnips, boiled meat, and pudding made from corn. Wampanoag tribesmen brought to the feast a basket filled with …popcorn!

Meanwhile, Chief Canonicus, sachem of the powerful Narragansetts, decided to challenge the Plymouth settlers. He sent a messenger who walked into the common house and threw on the table in front of the governor a bundle of arrows wrapped around with the skin of a rattlesnake. Squanto was away hunting, and Edward Winslow didn't understand what the messenger was saying. Captain Standish invited the messenger to stay at his house until Squanto was back, but the messenger refused. He had heard all sorts of tales about the 'Thunder Chief,' as the native people called Standish. For some reason many of them believed he had barrels full of deadly diseases buried under his cabin and could unleash them on his enemies.

The next morning Squanto returned and explained that the meaning of arrows wrapped in the snake skin was 'Come out and fight.' "Soon many arrows will fly in this village," he said. "People will die." But Bradford was not afraid. He tossed away the arrows and filled the snake skin with powder and shot. Handing it to Squanto, he said, "Take that to the Narragansetts. Tell them we've done them no harm, but we are ready to fight if they come."
This warning was enough. Sachem Canonicus backed off.

Meanwhile, the Plymouth settlers wondered who told the Narragansetts about the barrels under Myles Standish's house. Indeed, there were barrels stored under the house, but they were filled with food for the colony, not with deadly diseases.

Soon the mystery was solved. Hobbamock, Chief Massasoit's right hand man, overheard Squanto telling other tribesmen about the plague under Standish's house. It turned out Squanto collected 'gifts' from his fellow native people for 'protecting' them from the white man's god who could release the plague on them at any moment.

"Tisquantum sought his own ends and played his own game to enrich himself," wrote Bradford. Indeed, now called 'the tongue of the English,' Squanto grew wealthy and started thinking that he would make a better chief of the Wampanoag Confederacy than Massasoit. So he came up with a scheme to have the colonists attack Massasoit.

Early in the summer of 1622, the colonists were told that the Massachusetts tribes were planning to attack a new colony that had been established at Wessagussett, and then attack Plymouth itself. Captain Standish rushed to Wessagussett and attacked the local tribe, but, to his shame, he didn't find any evidence that the native people were hostile to Wessagussett colonists. Next Squanto arranged for himself and Standish to leave Plymouth on a trade mission. Just as they left the colony, a native man – wounded and bleeding – appeared before Governor Bradford claiming that Massasoit was coming to attack Plymouth and that he was a friend of Squanto wounded by Massasoit's warriors.

Bradford ordered the Mayflower cannon to be fired, hoping Standish could hear it. Standish heard it and returned. The colonists contacted Hobbamock who told them it was a hoax – Massasoit had no intention to attack Plymouth. He sent his wife to Massasoit's village and she confirmed that there were no preparations for war. Right away, Massasoit demanded that Squanto be executed for treason. He sent a messenger to Bradford. The messenger handed Bradford Massasoit's knife and a bundle of beaver fur in exchange for Squanto's life.
No need to send Squanto to Massasoit for execution, explained the messenger:
"Just cut off his head and hands and I will take them to the chief."
"It's not the manner of the English to sell a man's life at a price," responded Bradford.

Squanto continued working for the colonists as an interpreter, but one day he suddenly felt very sick. His nose was bleeding. He said he was going to die. According to Bradford, he asked "to pray for him, that he might go to the Englishmen's God in heaven. He left all his things to English friends, as remembrances of his love." Indeed, soon Squanto died. The settlers suspected that he was poisoned on the order of Massasoit who decided to execute Squanto by poison rather than risk a conflict with Governor Bradford.

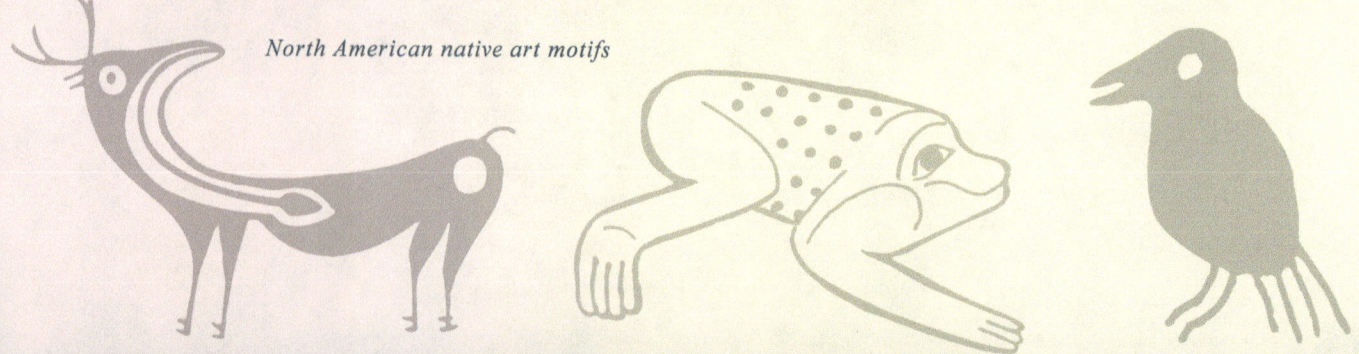

North American native art motifs

KING PHILIP
1638 – 1676

King Philip was a son of Massasoit. His birth name was Metacomet, but – as a gesture of good will – Massasoit asked Plymouth settlers to give his sons European names. His son Wamsutta was renamed Alexander, and Metacomet – Philip. After Massasoit's death, Wamsutta became the leader of the Wampanoag Confederacy. But in 1662 Wamsutta died, and Metacomet, or King Philip, became the Wampanoag chief. Wamsutta's death followed his meeting with the Plymouth colony assistant governor Josiah Winslow. King Philip was convinced that Winslow had poisoned his brother.

Colonists who knew King Philip described him as "a person of good understanding and knowledge." They believed he was a loyal friend, because on several occasions he helped English families who were friendly to him or to his father. Philip was fearless and principled.

In 1665, King Philip heard that a Wampanoag tribesman had spoken disrespectfully of his father, Massasoit. The offender's name was Assasamooyh and he was a Christian. According to native custom, whoever spoke ill of the dead was condemned to lose his life at the hand of the nearest relative of the dead. To avenge the insult, Philip – alone – crossed in a canoe to the island of Nantucket where Assasamooyh was visiting with the English colonists. Hearing that Philip was near, Assasamooyh rushed out of the house. But Philip spotted and chased him. Aasasamooyh escaped into the forest and that saved his life. Philip fell behind and later agreed to accept a heavy ransom from the colonists in exchange for the offender's life.

By the time Philip became the Wampanoag Chief, the New England colonists population was 65,000 persons, living in 110 towns. The native population was only 10,000, of which Wampanoags were fewer than 1000. To expand their farms, the English bought land from the local tribes, but the compensation received by the native people often consisted of small gifts, European goods, or even alcoholic beverages. Trying to fix this problem the colonial government passed a law prohibiting land purchases for trinkets, weapons, or alcohol, and all purchases had to be approved by a colonial court. But the damage had already been done.

As time went on, the Wampanoags resented the deals they had made with the colonists. In addition, farmers always cleared the forest and destroyed the habitat of the wild animals the Indians hunted, and the farmers' pigs and cattle trampled Indian cornfields. King Philip decided to stop land sales to the English for 7 years, but he needed money, so in 1665, grudgingly, he agreed to sell more land. All this contributed to a worsening of the tensions between the colonists and the New England native tribes.

In 1667, King Philip asked his secretary, John Sossamon, a Christian tribesman who had graduated from Harvard College, to help him write his will in English. Philip wanted to leave all his property to his baby son, but John Sossamon deceived him and wrote a will where all King Philip's property was left to... Sossamon! When Philip sent word to local tribal chiefs asking them to join him in an uprising against the colonists, Sossamon betrayed him once again. He overheard King Philip's conversations about the uprising and reported them to Winslow, hoping to be paid for that report. Winslow didn't believe him. Next, John Sossamon mysteriously disappeared. Soon his body was found in a pond, under the ice.

King Philip was ordered to appear before the colonial court and explain the uprising rumors and John Sossamon's death. Philip denied everything. In response Winslow ordered the Wampanoag to turn over their weapons – steel knives, axes, and flintlock muskets purchased from the English. Then, suddenly, an eyewitness appeared who claimed that Sossamon was murdered by three native warriors, including one of King Philip's advisors. In June 1675 the English called a jury of 12 Englishmen and six native elders, the accused were convicted and hanged. That was a violation of the treaty between the English and the native tribes which stipulated that native people should be tried and punished only by their own tribes.

King Philip's War breaks out

Outraged, Philip summoned his allies to a council of war. The plan was to buy more guns from the Dutch and the French, to talk the 'praying Indians' – the native people who had converted to Christianity – into being neutral, and to bribe the Mohawks and the Narragansetts into joining King Philip's anti-colonial league. The medicine men built a fire, and called on the great Spirit of the war path. One by one the warriors walked to the fire, and threw some of their most valued treasures into the flames – furs, shell-embroidered belts, rare feathers - as sacrifices to the spirit of war.

The medicine men also predicted that whichever party shed the first blood, would be defeated. Because of that, for some days Wampanoag warriors burned the houses and killed the cattle of the colonists, but avoided harming the settlers. Then, one day, in a clash over cattle, a farmer shot and wounded a Wampanoag tribesman. A few days later, on Sunday, the Wampanoag attacked and slaughtered the colonists in the town of Swansea as they were leaving church. Then they burned down the town. King Philip's war began. The Massachusetts authorities asked King Philip for peace negotiations, but Philip replied, "Your governor is a subject of King Charles of England. I shall not negotiate with a subject. I shall discuss peace only with the King, my brother. When he comes, I am ready."

Colonial troops from the Massachusetts and Connecticut towns, joined by the Mohegans – the enemies of the Wampanoags – marched to King Philip's camp in Mount Hope, but Philip fled to Pocasset, a vast marsh, overgrown with hemlocks, brambles and the moldering trunks of fallen trees. The English did not dare to follow him through the deep, black mire. They built a fort and kept up a siege for two weeks, hoping to starve him out of his hiding place. Philip, however, managed to escape with a band of his warriors, ready to continue the uprising.

A full eclipse of the moon that occurred in the New England area on June 27, 1675 was interpreted by his medicine men as a good omen. King Philip's warriors raided towns and farms, killing adults, taking children away as slaves, and burning houses and fields. In order to spread fear among the colonists, the Wampanoag warriors ambushed individual farmers, shooting men in the fields and women in the kitchen. Colonists were terror-stricken: Their enemy was swift and invisible.

"Indian war dance," a 1913 photo, Winnipeg

The Wampanoags didn't hesitate to attack the armed forces of the settlers as well. Massachusetts Bay Colony sent a company of 90 soldiers, with 18 wagons, to Deerfield, Massachusetts, to collect grain left behind by fleeing farmers. On their way back, the soldiers let go of their muskets to pick wild grapes by a forest stream. In an instant hundreds of bullets and arrows came whizzing and 700 native warriors appeared from the surrounding thickets. All the English were killed except seven. The stream by which they fell became known as the Bloody Brook. Gunshots were heard by Captain Mosely of Deerfield, who rushed to the scene with a company of 70 armed colonists. Native tribesmen called him 'Paleface-with-two-heads', because he hung his wig on a nearby bush while he fought. Mosely's militia was soon reinforced by the Mohegans and English troops. The attackers were defeated, but the victory was short-lived. Soon Deerfield was raided and burned down by King Philip's allies.

The Narragansett tribe, though not participating in the uprising, agreed to give refuge to some Wampanoags. Governor Winslow demanded that they be handed over. The Narragansett refused. Then Winslow sent the colonial militia and two bands of Pequot and Mohegan Indians, to storm the Narragansett fort which was located in the middle of the Great Swamp near Kingston, Rhode Island. An Indian guide led them to the fort over the frozen swamp, and in the battle that followed, 600 Narragansetts, including women and children perished. This was a huge blunder. The Narragansetts immediately joined the war on the side of King Philip. Philip sent wampum – strings of beads made from shells – as presents to his principal chiefs, and congratulated them on the success of the uprising.

WAMPUM

'Wampum' is a Wampanoag word referring to the white beads native people made from whelk shells and purple beads made from the shells of quahog clams. Most wampum was produced by the Narragansetts. Belts made of wampum were used by the tribes of the Eastern Woodlands to record their treaties with one another. These beads were also a trade good – a form of money – until English settlers used their manufacturing technologies to produce wampum belts in huge quantities, causing wampum to lose its value.

In February of 1676, the town of Lancaster, 30 miles from Boston, was attacked by a large band of warriors under Philip. 42 colonists fled to the house of a local resident, Mary Rowlandson. Most of them perished. Mary and her three children were taken prisoners. Her younger daughter died from wounds. Mary and her surviving kids were sold to Weetamoo, the wife of Philip's dead brother, and the sunksqua (or female sachem) of Pocasset. After 11 months of captivity Mary Rowlandson was ransomed for £20, contributed by the women of Boston, and wrote a memoir where she described life among the Wampanoags and meeting King Philip himself. Philip often visited Weetamoo and was kind to Mary. "Philip spoke to me," wrote Mary, "to make a shirt for his little boy, which I did, for which he gave me a shilling... Afterward he asked me to make a cap for his boy, for which he invited me to dinner. I went, and he gave me a pancake." One of Philip's warriors came back from a raid on a colonial town with some plunder. "He came to me," wrote Mary, "and asked me if I would like to have a Bible" taken in the raid.

Things looked good for King Philip until, in 1676, he led his warriors to New York to ask Mohawk tribes for help. The Iroquois-speaking Mohawks were old enemies of the Algonquin tribes. To provoke the Mohawks to join the war, King Philip – reportedly – staged a 'false flag' attack. He shot three Mohawk warriors, and blamed the English for the murder. But one of his victims lived to tell the truth. The Mohawks sided with the English and drove King Philip back to New England. The losses King Philip's forces suffered during the clash with the Mohawks, decided the outcome of the war. Many hundreds of King Philip's warriors surrendered to the English.

'Death of King Philip' by Frank O. Small

'FALSE FLAG'

A 'false flag' operation or attack is a harmful action performed in a way that places the blame on someone other than the person or group actually responsible for it. 'Planting' fake evidence is a form of false flag operation.

To avoid being recognized, King Philip cut off his hair and was hiding in the swamps, but the colonists discovered his camp, and seized his wife and 9-year-old son. Philip narrowly escaped capture. He was quoted as having said "My heart is broken. I am ready to die." Nevertheless, when one of his warriors advised surrender, Philip killed him on the spot. Then a brother of the slain warrior, a Christian tribesman by the name of John Alderman, led two teams of English and native fighters by a secret trail to Philip's camp in the Assawompset Swamp near Providence. Avenging the death of his brother, Alderman tracked down Philip, shot him dead, and cut off his head and hands to keep as trophies. King Philip's wife and 9-year-old son were sold into slavery by the English and sent to the West Indies. This happened to many other native people as well, because Governor Winslow declared all the people of the local tribes to be guilty of war crimes, whether they had taken part in the war or not. John Alderman charged the colonists money to see King Philip's head until he sold it to Plymouth Colony for 30 shillings. The head was displayed on a pike at the entrance of the Plymouth fort for 20 years.

'Settlers attacked by Indians' by F.O.C.Darley

Pontiac
1714 – 1769

"Pontiac" by John Mix Stanley

Pontiac grew up in an Ottawa tribe close to Fort Detroit. In the 1740s, he became the Ottawa war chief. During the French and Indian War (1754–1763), Pontiac supported the French against the British and their native allies, but the British won the war and took over Quebec. For the native people it was a disaster.

The French were fair in trade, and respectful of the native customs and lifestyle. When the Indian chiefs visited French forts or trading posts, they were treated with great pomp and ceremony. The French distributed European goods and tobacco as gifts to the Indians to keep them interested in cooperation, and didn't mind supplying them with guns and ammunition for hunting. In contrast, the British were demanding and unforgiving. They canceled gifts, calling them 'bribes,' banned sales of guns to the Indians, and opened sales of rum – the "fire-water" as native people called it – that caused addiction and disrupted native society. The growing tide of English immigration pushed the Indians from their lands. The French encouraged Canada's native people to rise up against the British.

In 1760, as English garrisons started to replace the French in the surrendered forts, a British officer, Major Rogers, brought a company of British rangers to Fort Detroit. Approaching Detroit, he was stopped by Pontiac's warriors who told Rogers that "the lord and ruler of this country" wished to speak with him. Pontiac soon appeared and asked Rogers: "What is your business in my country, and how dare you enter it without my permission?" Rogers said he had brought soldiers to take over the fort. Pontiac responded, "You can not go farther until Pontiac leaves your path." Then he added, "Englishman, I shall stand in your path till morning. In the meantime if your warriors are cold or hungry, the hands of my people are open to you." Then he and his chiefs slipped silently through the dark forest to their camp.

The following day Pontiac came again, offering to smoke the pipe of peace with Major Rogers. Pontiac realized that to stand in the way of the British, he needed far more preparation. He was also impressed with Rogers' courage and commitment to his duty.

Years later, Major Rogers sent to the chief a bottle of rum. "What if it's poisoned?" worried Pontiac's advisors, but Pontiac replied: "I did not spare the life of a man who would today poison me," and he drank the rum without hesitation. Major Rogers was also impressed, and described his meetings with Pontiac in these words: "I had several conferences with the chief in which he displayed great strength of judgment and a thirst for knowledge. He puts on an air of majesty and princely grandeur, and is greatly honored and revered by his subjects."

With every year Pontiac's influence grew. Like many native leaders, he realized that the Indians had become dependent on European manufacturing and farming. They had given up their bows and arrows and had to have guns to hunt. They accepted corn and smoked meats in winter because French and English farms produced much more than native crop patches. They bought many essentials from white traders: Winter clothes, blankets, iron tools, household goods. A native 'prophet,' Neolin, from the Delaware tribes, started a religious revival movement which called on the native people to break away from the influence of white culture and go back to their native lifestyle. Many of Pontiac's followers embraced the teaching of Neolin, but Pontiac knew there was no winning against the British with stone-age weapons like the bow and arrow. Even horses had been introduced to native tribes by white people. Were hunting or fighting even possible without a horse anymore? Pontiac knew the native tribes could not ignore or defeat European settlers and their culture. He focused on a smaller goal – to replace the British with the French.

HORSES

Horses were brought to the North American continent by Spanish conquistadors in the 16th century. By 1525 the Spanish started breeding horses in Mexico. Some horses escaped and adapted to life in the wild. The word 'mustang' comes from the Spanish 'mestengo' - a stray horse. Native tribes in Mexico learned horse training as well, and in 1680, during the uprising of the Pueblo tribes against the Spanish, native people captured large numbers of horses and started bartering them to tribes from the Great Plains. By the 18th century native people across North America came to rely on horses for transportation, war, and hunting, especially for hunting buffalo.

In April of 1763, signal fires were lit on mountain tops. Pontiac called together a war council where he said:
"It is important for us, my brothers, that we throw out from our lands this nation which seeks only to destroy us. We no longer receive supplies the way we received them from our brothers, the French... Therefore, my brothers, we must all swear to destroy the enemy, and wait no longer. They are few in numbers, and we can accomplish it. The French are all defeated, so who will become our Lords? A proud, imperious, childish, and arrogant band. The French were friends with us. They studied our language and customs, wore our clothes, married our daughters, traded honestly, and supplied things we needed. They never mistreated us, they respected our chiefs and elders and called us their children..."

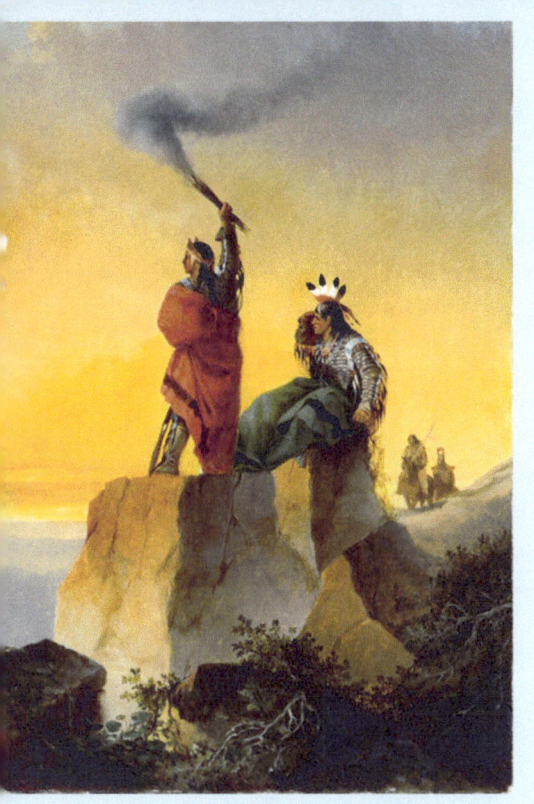

"Signal" by John Mix Stanley

Pontiac began planning a surprise attack on Fort Detroit. He called on his allies to attack other English forts on the same day. Then the native warriors would burn the English farms and settlements. Pontiac sent messengers carrying the war belt of wampum and a tomahawk, to the different tribes, and many pledged to take part in the war. The plan was kept secret to the very end. Up to the moment of the attack native warriors were supposed to show up at British trading posts, as usual, bartering for tobacco, gunpowder, and rum.

Detroit was founded by the French as an Indian trading post in 1701. By the mid 18th century it had 2500 French inhabitants, living on farms on both sides of the Detroit River. The fort in the center of the settlement protected about a hundred houses, surrounded by a 25-feet-high palisade with fortified wooden towers at each corner, and at two gateways. The garrison held 120 soldiers, plus about forty workers and fur-traders.

Pontiac's plan was to arm his warriors with guns cut short so that they could be hidden under their blankets and enter Fort Detroit pretending they came for a council with Major Gladwyn, the commander of the fort.

"Gifts for the Indians" by Alfred Jacob Miller

Then he planned to make a speech, and offer Gladwyn a peace belt of wampum. This belt was embroidered with white beads on one side and green beads on the other. Turning the belt from the white to the green side was to be the signal of attack. Also, Indian women would come to the fort in advance with guns and tomahawks hidden under their blankets, pretending to sell baskets. This way, inside the fort, the warriors would be well supplied with weapons.

However, the day before the planned attack, a white farmer saw some tribesmen filing off their guns to make them short and sent a word to Major Gladwyn. Also, an Indian woman who embroidered moccasins for Gladwyn came and warned him about the attack. And, finally, someone from Pontiac's allies betrayed him. As a result, Gladwyn knew all the details of Pontiac's plan. On May 7, when Pontiac entered Fort Detroit accompanied by 60 warriors, he instantly knew something had gone wrong. British soldiers were armed and ready for action. The shops were closed and the traders were armed to the teeth. Pontiac, however, moved on, and entered the council room, where Gladwyn and his officers, all well armed, waited for him.
"Why," asked Pontiac, "do I see so many men with guns standing in the street?"
"To keep them from idleness," replied the English commander.

Pontiac made his speech, but just as he lifted the peace belt he held in his hand, as if about to turn it over, Gladwyn gave a signal. The English drummers who stood outside the door beat the signal to charge. Some British officers drew their swords. Pontiac got the message. He laid the peace belt on the table white side up. Presents were exchanged, and the meeting was closed – with hand-shakes! The gates were opened, and Pontiac and his warriors left.

"Henry Gladwyn" by John Hall

"Siege of Fort Detroit" by Frederic Remington; Right: "Pontiac" – a 19th-century engraving

At this point Pontiac had nothing to lose, so he tried to capture the fort in an open attack. A large war party of 900 Ottawas and their allies rode up to Fort Detroit and kept up an incessant fire for several hours. They shot burning arrows into the fort, setting buildings on fire. For days Pontiac's warriors continued the attacks, but couldn't capture the fort. Meanwhile their allies in other areas burned to the ground dozens of white settlements and farms and succeeded in taking around 10 British forts. The forts were wooden and their garrisons consisted of an officer and 10-20 soldiers. The British didn't expect an Indian uprising: Since the French had been on good terms with the native tribes, the British expected to be treated with equal friendliness.

As the siege of Fort Detroit continued, Pontiac ran out of food and other supplies and his warriors threatened to leave. Pontiac met with the French farmers along the Detroit River and arranged with them to supply his people with corn and meat. He had no money to pay for these purchases, so he made out notes promising to pay for them at some future time. Written on birch bark, these notes had a symbol representing the item that was purchased, and Pontiac's signature – a pictograph of an otter, the totem (ancestor / guardian spirit) of his family.
He kept his word and always paid on these notes. To prevent wasteful use of supplies, Pontiac hired a Canadian Frenchman to guard the storehouse and give out rations for the day to Pontiac's warriors. He had two interpreters – one to read the letters he received, and one to write for him. For security, these interpreters were not allowed to talk to each other.

"Dividing the estate of a dead chief" by Joseph Henry Sharp

Some French Canadians encouraged Pontiac in his war, promising that the French king would send him help. But week after week passed and no help came. Many French farmers, however, only pretended to be on Pontiac's side. Actually, under the cover of night, they smuggled cattle, sheep, and hogs to the garrison of Detroit and reported the movements of Pontiac's bands.

Late in July, Pontiac learned that 22 barges carrying large supplies of food and ammunition and 300 English soldiers had reached Fort Detroit, protected by a dense fog. The next day Pontiac's spies brought him word that the English were mounting an attack on his camp. Pontiac ambushed the British and defeated them by a bridge across a creek that was later named Bloody Run. Hearing the news of this victory, more native warriors joined Pontiac's force and the siege of Fort Detroit continued.

Most British boats trying to deliver supplies to the fort were captured by Pontiac's warriors in birch-tree canoes. All prisoners were killed and their bodies floated down the river to terrify the defenders of the fort. One small schooner with 10 sailors on board managed to break through the siege. When the Ottawas stormed it and climbed on board, the first mate pretended to give an order to the sailors: "Blow up the schooner!" Ottawas knew enough English to understand his words and jumped off the boat.

At some point the British started sending to Detroit larger ships armed with multiple guns. They sank birch-tree canoes and, sailing against the wind and the current, fired on Pontiac's camp. Pontiac had two large rafts tied together and loaded with birch bark and pitch pine.

Vintage prints: "The Fire Rafts in Detroit River" and "Attack on the Schooner"

The rafts were set on fire and floated down the river to burn the British ships by the Fort. But the current carried the rafts toward the middle of the river and past the Fort.

In October, when the hunting season came, Pontiac's warriors wanted to return to their villages. Some of the bands deserted Pontiac and made peace with the English. They lied saying that Pontiac had forced them to fight. Pontiac sent a messenger to the commander of the French garrison at Fort Chartres, in the Illinois country, asking for help. In his response, the commander told Pontiac the truth: The French in America were now the subjects of the English king, and so could not fight against the British. Disappointed, Pontiac decided to end the siege. He sent a letter to Major Gladwin in Fort Detroit, saying that he was now ready to bury the hatchet, and forget the past. Major Gladwin blamed the war on the French, who – he thought – had used and betrayed Pontiac. So he sent Pontiac a friendly reply. A few days later Pontiac left the Detroit area.

BURY THE HATCHET

The expression 'to bury the hatchet' comes from a Native American ceremony of making peace by burying two tomahawks – for each of the sides in the war – as a symbol of putting away weapons and ending the hostilities.

The British thought they won the war, but even though Pontiac had a huge influence on many tribes, native people didn't wage war under one commander, the way the Europeans did. Many of Pontiac's allies continued raiding English settlements and forts and many more battles were fought. Enraged by the Indian raids against the civilians, frontier men organized militias that started raiding peaceful Indian villages in revenge. The British commanders offered money to frontiersmen for Indian prisoners and scalps, and even discussed measures 'uncivilized' by their own standards, such as sending the Indians blankets infected with smallpox, or fighting them with bloodhounds instead of soldiers. As winter approached, most native tribes found they had no food, and no help from the French or the British, on whom they had relied for years. They suffered bitter hardships. Most of them abandoned Pontiac's cause.

Out of many chiefs whose bands chose resistance against the British, Pontiac was singled out by the British commanders as the leader of the Indian uprising. Because of that, Pontiac's influence among the native tribes steadily grew, even after Pontiac's war was over.

European settlers viewed Pontiac only as a bitter and savage enemy. Their hatred for him deepened in 1767, when Pontiac was accused of the murder of Betty Fisher, a 7-year-old English girl from a local farm. Her parents were killed in a raid by Pontiac's warriors. Betty was taken captive and spent about a year in Pontiac's camp. One day she came to Pontiac's campfire to warm herself up, but she felt sick, and accidentally soiled Pontiac's blanket stretched on the ground. Eyewitnesses said that Pontiac grabbed the girl and threw her into the river. Then he ordered one of his men, a Frenchman, to drown her. Pontiac was summoned to Detroit by the investigators, and would have been arrested, but the Frenchman who had drowned Betty escaped, and the investigation was stopped.

In 1769 Pontiac visited the St. Louis area to see some of his former French allies and traders. When he walked through the forest after the feast, he was ambushed and killed by an Illinois native warrior, who was avenging the death of his uncle, Black Dog, stabbed to death by Pontiac in 1766.

"The Ojibway maiden disclosing Pontiac's plot" by John Tinkey
Right: Death of Pontiac;
$10 "Indian Head" US coin, 1908

SEQUOYAH
1770 – 1843

No native tribe in North America had a written language. When Europeans settled on their lands, many native people learned English, and sought European-style education. However, their own traditions, lore, and history remained unrecorded. There was no way to write them down in the native languages. Sequoyah created the first native North American writing system – the 'syllabary' for his native language, Cherokee.

Sequoyah was born in the Cherokee town of Tuskegee, Tennessee. Sequoyah's dad was either white or of mixed race (native-white). He was a fur trader. Sequoyah's mother was a daughter of the Cherokee chief of Echota who ran a trading post – a store. According to native custom, Sequoyah was raised by his mother. He never went to school and never learned English. At home they spoke only Cherokee. As a kid, Sequoyah suffered a knee injury and it became clear that he would never become a hunter, a farmer, or a warrior. His mother taught him trading. For fun he built miniature models of Cherokee houses. As a teenager Sequoyah displayed a talent for engineering, constructing a dairy shed for his mother's cows, with milk troughs and skimmers of his own design.

Above: Portrait of Sequoyah by Charles Bird King, 1828, and Sequoyah's Cherokee syllabary

a	e	i	o	u	v [ə̃]
D a	R e	T i	Ꮼ o	Oʻ u	i v
S ga ka	Ւ ge	Ꭹ gi	A go	J gu	E gv
ov ha	Ꭾ he	Ꭿ hi	Ꮀ ho	Ꮁ hu	Ꮂ hv
W la	᧚ le	P li	G lo	M lu	Ꮏ lv
ᏑᎷ ma	Ꮊ me	H mi	Ꮊ mo	Ꮊ mu	
Θ na hna G nah	Ꮑ ne	ɦ ni	Z no	Ꮕ nu	0 nv
Ꮖ qua	Ꮙ que	Ꮖ qui	Ꮜ quo	Ꮝ quu	Ꮞ quv
Ꮞ s Ꮞ sa	4 se	b si	Ꮠ so	Ꮡ su	R sv
Ꮣ da W ta	S de Ꮦ te	Ꮧ di Ꮨ ti	V do S du	Ꮬ dv	
Ꮩ dla Ꮭ tla	L tle	C tli	Ꮰ tlo	Ꮱ tlu	P tlv
G tsa	Ꮴ tse	Ꮵ tsi	K tso	Ꮷ tsu	Cʼ tsv
G wa	ꮿ we	Θ wi	Ꮼ wo	9 wu	6 wv
Ꮿ ya	ꮿ ye	Ꭹ yi	Ꮿ yo	G yu	B yv

When Sequoyah turned 15, Cherokee custom required that he 'make his medicine.' The ritual included spending a couple days alone in the forest, waiting for a message from the Great Spirit. One night Sequoyah had a dream that a toad hopped into the fold of his shirt, which was the Great Spirit's sign that the little animal was to be his mysterious protector throughout his life. Having returned home, Sequoyah made a 'medicine bag' from the skin of a toad, and filled it with medicinal herbs. He carried it with him always.

When his mother died, Sequoyah took over her trading business. All of a sudden he was thrown into daily contact with English colonists and fur-traders who were now swarming into the Cherokee lands. He was learning English, and for the first time he held in his hands the white man's 'talking leaves,' as native people called printed pages.

Native tribes used a variety of symbols carved on wood, bark, stone or animal skins to communicate ideas, but they were not enough to record the words of the native languages. Sequoyah realized that his people needed a writing system, but he didn't know yet how to approach that task. He started by cutting the marks of his tribe on rocks and trees. Then he began to paint figures of animals, and of people, scenes of hunting and daily life, on bark or animal skins, using charcoal, red ocher, and dyes extracted from the roots of plants.
His drawings told stories. It was a form of picture writing. Sequoyah became so skilful in his art that crowds of spectators gathered daily to watch him paint.

Sequoyah also painted a deer-skin ceremonial robe, which was so impressive that his tribe's chief, Atakullakulla, ordered a dance in his honor. To the music of drum and rattle, one after another, Cherokee warriors stepped toward the campfire and danced. Each man told a story of his victory in war or a success during a hunt, and threw a gift for Sequoyah — paint, wire, arrow-heads, and wampum — on the bearskin spread on the ground.

Vintage books for kids about Sequoyah

Meanwhile, Sequoyah was looking for more ways to express his creative ideas. From white traders he learned how to make jewelry, creating necklaces and earrings from silver coins. His work was in great demand by both native people and white settlers. Money and praise flowed in fast. Sequoyah fell in love with one of the native girls who came to buy his jewelry, and their marriage was planned. His next step was to learn the craft of a blacksmith. White traders introduced native farmers to iron farming tools, and the demand for them was growing. Sequoyah designed and built his own forge and bellows, and soon he was manufacturing rakes, spades, and all sorts of metal tools with superior workmanship. His spurs and bridle bits were especially popular, because Sequoyah decorated them with silver.

"Indians playing cards" by John Mix Stanley

Sequoyah wanted to sign his name on the iron items he sold, and, again, he faced the same problem – there was no way to write his name in his native language. He asked a white friend, Mr. Lowrey, to put his name on a piece of paper, and Lowrey wrote Sequoyah's English name – George Guess. From it Sequoyah made a stamp to mark his work. He became a hero in his tribe.

But success and popularity had a negative effect on Sequoyah. His trading post became a party place where Cherokee warriors and traders gathered to socialize and drink whisky and rum. Sequoyah fell under their influence and for months he was drunk every day, spending all his money on 'fire water' as native people called alcohol. Fortunately, his friend Mr. Lowrey made an effort to talk Sequoyah out of this destructive behavior. He took Sequoyah to his own log house and lectured him about the value of Sequoyah's talent which he was ruining and about Sequoyah's great importance for his tribe and clan. Sequoyah listened to him and broke away from the influence of his drinking friends. Instead he started spending time with the older and wiser men of the tribe. Among them he heard conversations about a magic power possessed by the white man – the power to make curious marks on paper – such as those with which Mr. Lowrey had written his name. Sequoyah didn't view writing as a magical power. He viewed it as art that could be practiced by native people as well as by whites. Sequoyah announced that he would teach his people to 'talk on paper.' Cherokee elders only laughed at his words.

Sequoyah, however, was not discouraged. On thin sheets of birchwood bark, he painted pictures, each representing the name of some natural object. These were pictographs – a system, where every word in the language had a character or symbol. But soon Sequoyah gave up the idea of pictographs. He realized that he had accumulated so many symbols, he couldn't remember them all. Then he tried a different approach – a symbol would stand for an idea, not a word. But this system didn't seem to work either. By 1821 Sequoyah established that there were 86 syllables that made words of the Cherokee language, and started looking for characters to represent them.

Trading some silver ornaments for sheets of wrapping paper, he cut and bound the paper into a copybook. He also purchased from a fur trader a few leaves torn out of a Bible and an old English spelling book. He could not read a word on the 'talking leaves,' but, studying the distinct shapes of English, Greek, and Hebrew characters, he picked some of them for the Cherokee 'syllabary.'

While Sequoyah was absorbed in his work, the world around him was changing. White settlers started seizing lands which had been reserved for the Cherokees by a treaty with the government. Armed clashes and open warfare became part of everyday life. The US government was pushing the Cherokees to sell their lands and move West, beyond the Mississippi River.

Above: Early 20th-century photos of Cherokee girls
Left: "Sequoyah and his daughter Ayoka" – a diorama at the Sequoyah Birthplace Museum in Vonroe, TN

It occurred to Sequoyah that having a written language could help unify the Cherokee clans and give them a new sense of independence and pride. To test his work, Sequoyah started teaching his 6-year-old daughter, Ayoka, symbols and sounds of his syllabary, and soon the girl was able to read and write in Cherokee! Sequoyah was eager to share his work with others, but nobody believed him that he could write in Cherokee, not even Mr. Lowrey. Sequoyah invited Lowrey to his house and asked him to dictate a couple sentences in English. Lowrey did, and Sequoyah wrote down his words in Cherokee characters. Then he called Ayoka who spoke no English, and asked her to read what he had written. She read back the sentences quickly and easily. Lowrey was stunned.

It took 10 years for the Cherokee people to accept Sequoyah's ideas. Even Sequoyah's wife believed that writing was a form of witchcraft! She was so afraid that she burned some of Sequoya's birch tree bark writings. Cherokee elders distrusted anything that came from the white man. Sequoyah and Ayoka were seized and charged with practicing witchcraft. Their clan chief separated the father and the daughter and ordered them to exchange messages using Sequoyah's invention. After Sequoyah proved that writing worked, the chiefs agreed to a public test of the new alphabet. Sequoyah was to teach a few teenagers to read and write in Cherokee. After studying the writing system for 3 days, the young men were called before the elders, and in the presence of a huge crowd they wrote and read sentences dictated either by one of the elders or by spectators.

The Cherokee Phoenix newspaper in Cherokee and English

That was the moment of great victory for Sequouah. Cherokees were in awe that one of their own people had been able to achieve this for his tribe. So many young people wanted to learn reading and writing that Sequoyah couldn't teach them all. Schools were opened and textbooks were compiled. Part of Sequoyah's tribe had already abandoned their ancestral lands and settled in Arkansas. Sequoyah moved to Arkansas and taught Cherokees there. While he was away from his family, he wrote letters in Cherokee to his daughter. Then he went to the eastern tribes, carrying a sealed envelope with a speech by one of the Arkansas Cherokee chiefs. By reading it, he convinced the eastern Cherokee tribes to adopt his writing system as well. In 1828, Sequoyah joined a Cherokee delegation that went to Washington DC to negotiate a treaty for land in the Indian Territories of the West. In Washington, a well-known painter, Charles Bird King, made a portrait of Sequoyah with the syllabary in his hand. By 1830, 90% of Cherokees could read and write in their own language. Sequoyah's syllabary was used to translate the Bible into Cherokee. **The Cherokee Phoenix** became the first bilingual newspaper in North America. It was published in both English and Cherokee.

Meanwhile, Sequoyah was disturbed by the constant warfare between Georgia Cherokees, the state government, and the invading settlers. He moved from Georgia to Arkansas. In Arkansas he heard of a lost tribe of the Cherokees who were supposedly living farther to the West, maybe in Mexico. One day, when Sequoyah was over seventy years old, he decided to travel in search of that lost tribe, and invite them to join the Cherokee nation. With his son Teesy and a few students, he loaded a wagon with books and writing materials and left. He visited a number of Indian tribes and traveled to Mexico. On the trip to Mexico he got sick and died.

Today, in the towns of the Cherokee nation in Oklahoma, Cherokee is the co-official language with English. equoyah's syllabary can be seen on street signs and buildings. It is taught in schools in Oklahoma and North Carolina.

"Indian scout" by Afred Jacob Miller and the $1 Sequoyah coin

SACAJAWEA
1788 – 1812

Sacajawea became famous as an interpreter and guide for Meriwether Lewis and William Clark of the Lewis and Clark Expedition – a journey to explore western territories of the United States after the Louisiana Purchase of 1803.

Sacajawea – or Bird Woman – was born in the Lemhi Shoshone native tribe, also known as the Snake People – in present-day Idaho, near the Idaho-Montana border. The Shoshone Indians were hunter-gatherers. They lived in brush teepees, bred horses, hunted, and often moved from place to place.

"Sacajawea with Lewis and Clark"
by Newell Convers Wyeth

In the early 19th century Shoshones were desperately poor and constantly on the run, raided and robbed by the Hidatsa (also called the Minitaree) and other hostile tribes who were armed with guns supplied by white traders. Shoshones had only bows and arrows. The life of Shoshone women and girls was especially hard. "They treat their women with little respect and compel them to do all kinds of hard work," wrote Lewis after he visited Shoshone settlements. "Women collect the wild fruits and roots, cook, make all the clothes, collect wood and make their fires, build their lodges, and when they travel, pack the horses and take charge of all the baggage. In short, men do little except care for the horses, hunt, and fish..." Shoshone tribesmen "usually have many wives because they are needed to do the work. The man considers himself humiliated if he has to walk on foot. He leaves women to transport the baggage and children…and to walk if the horse is unable to carry additional weight." In other words, women's status was that of a slave. A husband could even sell his wife if she wasn't seen as useful.

When girls became teenagers, their fathers usually sold them into marriage, typically accepting horses as payment from the future husband. Sooner or later Sacajawea would have been sold. But when Sacajawea was 12, a band of Hidatsa warriors raided the camp of her clan. Most of her family was killed. Sacajawea was captured and sold as a slave to the Mandans, allies of the Hidatsa. After a while, a fur trader from Quebec, Toussaint Charbonneau, saw Sacajawea at a Mandan village and won her from her owner while gambling.

Charbonneau's mother was French, but his father was an Iroquois. Speaking French, English, and Iroquois, he lived with the Mandan and had an Indian wife called 'the Otter Woman' – another Shoshone captive purchased from the Hidatsa. Sacajawea became Charbonneau's second wife. Marrying a trader was considered prestigious among native people. Sacajawea was no longer a slave. She wore a fine embroidered deerskin dress and expensive shell jewelry. But her husband had a short temper and didn't hesitate to hit her if she failed to fulfill his orders.

Meanwhile, the Corps of Discovery, sent by President Thomas Jefferson and led by Lewis and Clark, arrived in the Mandan area and built Fort Mandan to stay through the winter of 1804–05. Lewis and Clark met Toussaint Charbonneau and considered hiring him as an interpreter for the trip up the Missouri River in the spring. When they heard that his wife Sacajawea spoke Shoshone, they invited Charbonneau and Sacajawea to join the expedition. When the Corps of Discovery reached the source of the Missouri River, they would sell the boats and Sacajawea would help them buy horses from the Shoshones – to continue the expedition on land.

*Above: "Fur trader's bride';
below: "Gambling Indians"
by John Mix Stanley*

At that time Sacajawea was expecting a baby, but even though a journey with a newborn all the way to the Pacific Ocean seemed a crazy idea, she was eager to visit her native land. She started coming every day to the fort, to help Lewis and Clark stock up on food supplies for the expedition. She cut buffalo meat into thin strips, dried it on the racks, and prepared pemmican – a mix of dried meat, cranberries, and beef fat. She sliced pumpkins and squashes into thin rings and then linked the rings into chains for drying. She sewed moccasins for the expedition. She also embroidered a sheet of doeskin with birds and flowers to serve as the coverlet for the cradle board of her soon-to-be-born baby.

The men of the expedition were friendly and sociable. Clark brought with him an enslaved African, York, who was helpful, funny, and popular with the natives. The Indians had never seen black people before and were convinced that York's skin was just painted black. York was promised freedom once the expedition was over, but, sadly, Clark never fulfilled his promise. Instead, he named a river after York, and once they came back from the journey, York was sold to another owner.

Two months before the start of the expedition, Sacajawea gave birth to a son – Jean-Baptiste (nicknamed Pompy by Clark). She carried him on her back in a traditional deerskin bag attached to a cradle board.

'Lewis and Clark at Three Forks' by Edgar S. Paxson

The baby was only 8 months old when the April sun broke up the ice on the Missouri River, and the Expedition – 31 men and Sacajawea with her baby – set out in pirogues, small canoes made from a single log. Whenever they stopped to trade with local tribes, the Indians were friendly. The presence of Sacajawea with a baby signaled to them that the Expedition was not a war party. Sacajawea taught Lewis and Clark native customs that helped them communicate with the local tribes. For instance, the ritual of meeting and greeting strangers in many tribes went like this: The local chief stepped forward, took off his cloak, and threw it in the air 3 times holding it by two corners. Then he spread it on the ground – an invitation to sit down. The strangers approached, everybody sat, took off their moccasins as a sign of good will, and smoked pipes in silence before starting a conversation.

On May 14, 1805, a boat steered by Toussaint Charbonneau nearly tipped over after a storm knocked down its sail. Charbonneau lost control of the boat and it instantly filled with water. Sacajawea, who was in the same boat, jumped in the river and swam to the shore with her baby. Then she noticed the journals and records of the expedition that spilled from their bags and floated on the water, being carried away by the rapid current. Leaving Jean-Baptiste on the shore, she plunged back into the river and managed to catch and collect most of the books and maps of the expedition. She also saved heir compass. In gratitude, a few days later, Lewis and Clark named a river in Montana the Sacajawea River.

"Clark on the Lower Columbia"
by Charles Marion Russell.

In June, when the Rocky Mountains came into view, Sacajawea became dangerously ill. Lewis, who was trained in medicine, tried various European and native medicines to help her recover. The Expedition members took daily care of her, in contrast to Charbonneau, who mostly ignored her and even demanded that she go gather wild apples and cook. The journals of Lewis and Clark show their sincere concern for Sacajawea – at this point they knew that she was perhaps the most valuable member of their team. Sacajawea felt better after drinking mineral water from a sulfur spring by the Great Falls.

Soon the Expedition approached the Shoshone country, and Sacajawea started recognizing features of landscape she remembered from her childhood. They passed Indian trails and abandoned camps. The snowy range of the Shining Mountains was nearer. Lewis and Clark raised US flags on the canoes, to indicate their identity. During their second day in the mountains Sacajawea noticed glimpses of fire in the woods. But it wasn't a camp fire. Shoshones had heard the gunshots of the Expedition members who went hunting and thought that their rifle-armed enemies, the Hidatsa, had arrived to attack them in the mountains. The Shoshone set fire to dry grass as a warning, and fled. Clark prohibited any further firing of the Expedition's guns. They had to make contact with the Shoshone tribes, purchase horses, leave their boats, and continue the journey on land.

Lewis led a team to look for the Shoshone. But Shoshones had never seen Europeans, and, spotting them, ran for their life. Finally, Lewis came across two Shoshone women who accepted from him some gifts – beads, paint, and a mirror. The contact with the Shoshones was made. Lewis and Clark purchased a few horses, but they needed many more, so they went to a Shoshone camp again. Following a ritual of hospitality, the Great Chief of the Salmon Eater Shoshone band invited Clark to sit on a white skin. Then they took off their moccasins, smoked a peace pipe, and Clark sent for Sacajawea to interpret the conversation. When she came, she was stunned: The chief was her brother! William Clark described Chief Cameahwait as "a man of influence, sense, and reserved manners, who appears to possess a great deal of sincerity."

Lewis and Clark were impressed with the Shoshones. "They are frank, communicative, fair in dealing, generous with the little they possess, extremely honest, and by no means beggarly," wrote Lewis. "Each individual is his own sovereign master, and acts from the dictates of his own mind...." The only criticism was that, "like all Indians, they frequently boast of heroic acts which they never performed." Cameahwait accepted the gift of a medal with the portrait of President Jefferson. Sacajawea gave her brother a tiny lump of sugar, and he said it was "the best thing he had ever tasted." They all enjoyed a feast together.

There were problems, however. Sacajawea learned that her people were afraid white men would eventually claim their land. They promised to help the explorers transport their baggage up the mountain where horses were waiting for them. But Sacajawea heard some of the tribesmen discussing a different plan. They would just leave, abandoning the explorers on the mountaintop. Sacajawea shared this information with her husband, but Charbonneau chose not to warn Lewis and Clark. He was angry that Lewis gave Sacajawea the best horse of the few they had purchased, and she rode, while he walked behind her on foot. Somehow Lewis learned of the deception, and rushed to talk with the Shoshone chiefs. This time, in exchange for the horses he offered to arm them with rifles. The chiefs agreed. Sacajawea was invited to stay with her tribe, but she declined.

Crossing the Rocky mountains was hard. The explorers had no idea how far they were from the Pacific Coast. They hoped to reach the ocean within days, but the journey lasted 4 months. The Expedition ran out of food and had to kill and eat their horses. They even ate candles made from animal fat. On the other side of the mountains Sacajawea taught the explorers how to cook camas roots – Indian hyacinth – which resembled sweet potatoes. She also made bread from wild sunflower seeds and bear grease. Native to the Americas, sunflowers had been cultivated by native peoples for thousands of years.

"Lewis and Clark reach the Shoshone camp led by Sacajawea". by Charles Marion Russell.

"Lewis and Clark meeting Indians at Ross' Hole" by Charles M. Russell (The expedition's Shoshone guide speaks Plains Sign Language with the Salish Indians.)

Finally Lewis and Clark achieved their goal: They reached the Pacific Ocean. Trading with the Clatsop Indians at the mouth of the Columbia River, Lewis and Clark saw a beautiful fur robe. They decided to buy it as a gift for President Thomas Jefferson. "One of the Indians had on a robe made of 2 sea otter skins," wrote Clark. "Their fur was more beautiful than any fur I had ever seen. Both Captain Lewis and myself tried to purchase the robe offering different items. Finally, we bought it for a belt of blue beads which the Squaw, the wife of our interpreter Charbonneau, wore around her waist."

"Bartering blue beads for otter robe" by N. Myrah

The explorers built a fort for the winter, and took turns traveling on a canoe to look at the nearby Pacific Ocean. When Sacajawea heard that a whale carcass had washed up on the ocean beach, she asked to go see the 'great water' and the 'monstrous fish.' Clark wrote that this was the only time Sacajawea ever asked for anything.

During the return trip, Sacajawea told Lewis and Clark to cross the Yellowstone River basin at a gap in the mountains that she knew of. Clark wrote in his journal: "The Indian woman who has been of great service to me as a pilot through this country recommends a gap in the mountain further to the south which I shall take." The gap was named the Bozeman Pass. Many years later engineers chose it as the best route for the Northern Pacific Railway.

When Sacajawea and Charbonneau returned from the expedition, William Clark invited them to St. Louis, Missouri, and they moved there in 1809. Clark wanted to help Sacajawea, and since Charbonneau was traveling, trying different jobs, Clark volunteered to take care of young Jean-Baptiste's education. Clark enrolled Jean-Baptiste in the Saint Louis Academy boarding school, and also asked Charbonneau and Sacajawea if he could adopt the boy. Around that time Sacajawea gave birth to a daughter, Lizette. However, a few months later, in 1812, Sacajawea fell ill and died. William Clark did adopt both of her kids. Lizette died as a child, but Jean-Baptiste was raised by William Clark, became a celebrity, and had a life full of adventures.

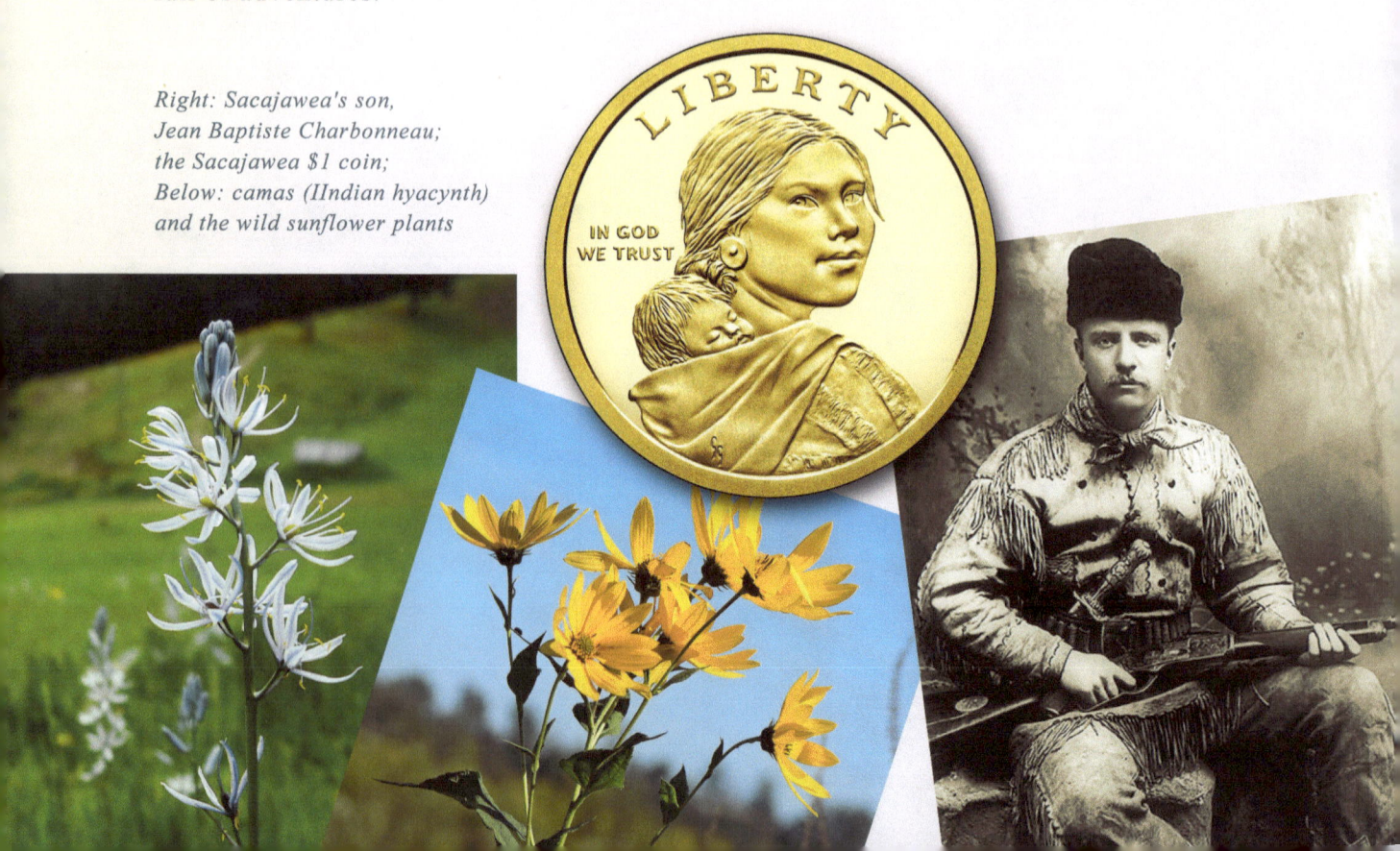

Right: Sacajawea's son, Jean Baptiste Charbonneau; the Sacajawea $1 coin; Below: camas (IIndian hyacynth) and the wild sunflower plants

Tecumseh
1768 – 1813

Tecumseh ('Shooting Star') was a Shawnee chief and an eloquent orator. He was born to a Shawnee father and a Creek mother in present-day Ohio. During the American Revolutionary War the Shawnees sided with the British and attacked American settlers in Kentucky. But they were defeated by the Kentucky militia. Their villages and crops were burned. Both Tecumseh's father and his older brother were killed in battles against American settlers. As a young man, Tecumseh vowed to keep the white men out of the Indian lands. The dream of his life was to form an Indian confederacy to unify the many different native tribes.

In 1800 the Indiana Territory was established, and General William Harrison was appointed governor. Harrison was popular with the Indians, but he failed to protect them from white settlers – who cheated the Indians in trade, claimed their land, and sold them alcohol that caused chronic drunkenness and crime. The price of furs fell because of commercial restrictions abroad, and many native clans plunged into poverty.

In 1805, Tecumseh's younger brother Tenskwatawa ('Open Door'), also known as the Shawnee Prophet, started a religious and cultural movement against European influence. He called on the Shawnees to stop drinking alcohol, reject European education (which he believed was witchcraft), forbid marriages between Indians and whites, ban European food, clothing, and goods, and to go back to their traditional native lifestyle. He told them that he had gone up into the clouds and visited the kingdom of the evil spirits. The evil spirits tortured whiskey drinkers by setting their mouths on fire. Many of Tenskwatawa's followers believed the Prophet was a miracle worker, and stopped drinking the 'fire water' sold to them by 'the children of the Evil Spirit."' Tecumseh used his brother's message to promote uniting the North-Western tribes. He started traveling from tribe to tribe inviting all to unite around his brother's divine mission. He said that the treaties between the Indians and the United States were void because the US forced each native tribe to sign its own land treaty with the government. However, the native land belonged to all tribes in common, said Tecumseh, and no part of it could be sold without the consent of all North American tribes.

Governor Harrison mocked Tenskwatawa as an impostor, challenging him to perform a miracle: "Tell the sun to stand still!" Meanwhile, astronomers predicted the eclipse of the sun that was to occur in the summer of 1806. Tenskwatawa learned from the white settlers when the eclipse was supposed to occur, and announced to the Shawnees that on a certain day he would bring darkness over the sun. The eclipse occurred as predicted. This produced a powerful effect on his followers.

In 1808, Tecumseh and Tenskwatawa founded Prophetstown, a village in present-day Indiana, which became the center of the Shawnee resistance and attracted thousands of Algonquin-speaking Indians from many tribes. In 1809 some tribes signed the Treaty of Fort Wayne, selling nearly 8 million acres on the Wabash river to the US government. Tribal leaders who were to receive payments from the government personally profited from the deal. They were – in effect – bribed. Tecumseh declared the treaty void, and threatened to kill any chief who signed it.

"Return those lands, and Tecumseh will be the friend of the Americans," he told Harrison, and, speaking of the US President he added, "As it's up to the Great Chief to determine this matter, I hope the Great Spirit will put enough sense into his head to direct you to give up this land. He is far away, and won't be injured by the war. He'll be sitting in his town and drinking his wine, while you and I will have to fight it out."

Tenskwatawa, Tecumseh's younger brother, by George Catlin

Tecumseh confronts Governor Harrison about the Treaty of Fort Wayne; right: Governor Harrison, later the 9th President of the United States

Tecumseh refused to negotiate on anything. According to one report, during a meeting between Harrison and the Shawnee chiefs, he spoke, standing, and then looked around to find a seat. There was no seat left, and he looked offended. Then one of Harrison's men offered him his seat next to the governor, saying, "Your father wishes you to sit by his side." Native people typically addressed the governor as 'Father,' while he addressed them as 'my children.' But Tecumseh refused the seat, and sat on the floor, saying, "The sun is my father, and the earth is my mother. I shall sit in his light and rest on her chest."

Realizing that the Americans would not back out of the Fort Wayne Treaty, Tecumseh went to Fort Malden in Upper Canada in 1810 to ask for British support in case of war. But the British didn't promise anything. They wanted Tecumseh to fight while they would cheer from across the border. Tecumseh traveled far and wide trying to unify the northern native tribes against the government. In 1811, the Indians in the Wabash region began occasional raids and attacks on white settlers. When Tecumseh met with Harrison to discuss the situation, he bragged to the governor that he had already built the confederacy of the northern tribes, and was planning to travel South to get the Southern tribes to join the anti-government alliance.

The Great Comet of 1811 over Europe

Indeed, soon Tecumseh went to Alabama. There he discovered that the Creek Indians were reluctant to join the war against the white settlers, with whom they were on good terms. In a burst of anger Tecumseh cried out, "Your blood is white, and no longer runs red like the rising sun. You don't fight because you are cowards. You don't believe the Great Spirit has sent me, but you shall believe it. I am going back to Detroit, and when I reach it, I'll tell everything to the Great Spirit, and I shall stamp my foot, and shake every house in your village."
In a most astounding coincidence, a few days later, on December 16, 1811, one of the strongest earthquakes in recorded American history shook the South of the United States!

It was a 7.2–8.2 magnitude earthquake with the epicenter in New Madrid on the Mississippi River. Many became convinced that Tecumseh was, indeed, the messenger of the Great Spirit.

But that wasn't all. Another famous astronomical marvel helped Tecumseh – the famous Great Comet of 1811. It was visible in the sky for many months – very bright, with a long sparkling tail. Since Tecumseh's name means 'Shooting Star' native people were convinced it was a sign from the Great Spirit. Tecumseh was now the hero of legends.

While Tecumseh traveled South, Tenskwatawa continued to recruit young warriors for the growing Indian army. He also started preparing for a battle, even though Tecumseh advised him to avoid any direct clash with the US Army. Knowing that Tecumseh was away, Harrison thought it was a good moment to crack down on Prophetstown. He sent Tenskwatawa a message accusing him of horse theft and of murders of white settlers in Illinois. He also demanded that all non-Shawnee residents should leave Prophetstown. Tenskwatawa promised that the horses would be returned, but ignored other accusations. For Harrison it was a good pretext to attack before Tecumseh returned. He gathered about 900 white volunteers and, together with some regular troops of the US Army set up a military camp near Prophetstown.

Tenskwatawa asked to negotiate, but at dawn on the day of his meeting with Harrison, he excited his warriors with war songs and dances, told them that the Great Spirit had promised them victory, and ordered a surprise attack on the US camp.

The Battle of Tippecanoe

He told the warriors that they would be protected from bullets by a powerful spell, and that his magic would make Americans drop their weapons and run in panic. Tenskwatawa's warriors tried to sneak inside the American camp, but failed. Harrison was familiar with Indian warfare tactics and expected the attack. His troops slept with rifles by their sides, and his guards kept the campfires burning despite the rain, to illuminate the camp. The battle that followed was known as the Battle of Tippecanoe. Tenskwatawa's forces were defeated.

According to one of the Shawnee war chiefs, retreating warriors confronted Tenskwatawa who stayed far away from the battle. "You are a liar!" they said. "You told us the white people would all die or be struck with madness, but actually they were all in clear mind and fought like devils." Tenskwatawa blamed the disaster on his wife, saying that during his incantations, his wife touched the sacred vessels and broke the spell. Nobody believed this. The Indian warriors deserted, Tenskwatawa fled, and Harrison's army burned Prophetstown to ashes. Tenskwatawa's authority as a prophet was destroyed. Tecumseh was furious at his brother, and even threatened to kill him. The confederacy he had built fell apart.

Meanwhile, the British and the Americans were about to fight the War of 1812. British authorities in Canada sent messengers to all the Indian tribes in and around the Indiana Territory, bringing them arms and gifts – and asking them to become allies of Great Britain. Tecumseh and his warriors joined the British immediately. When American General William Hull crossed into Canada, Tecumseh's native troops had a few clashes with the Americans. Tecumseh intercepted Hull's mail, and learned that the Americans were afraid of being cut off from their supply routes. Tecumseh and the British troops did precisely what Hull was predicting. Two days later, Hull recrossed the river to Detroit and left Canada. Next, Tecumseh and the British besieged Detroit and it surrendered without any resistance. After the surrender, British general Brock took off his red silk sash, and publicly gave it to Tecumseh. Tecumseh, however, gave it to one of his best warriors, saying, "I can't wear such a mark of distinction when an older and better warrior than myself is present."

"Tecumseh meets British general Isaac Brock"
by Charles William Jefferys

Next, Tecumseh and his warriors joined British General Henry Procter to besiege the American Fort Meigs in Ohio. The siege failed, but Tecumseh's warriors captured a number of American prisoners and started killing them. Tecumseh, who never allowed torture or murder of prisoners, stopped his warriors, and asked General Procter, who stood looking on, "Why do you permit this outrage?"
"Your Indians could not be controlled," replied Proctor, trembling with fear.
Tecumseh was furious. "Get out of here, coward!" he told Procter. "You are not fit to command men. Go and put on a skirt, and sit with the women, where you belong."

Tecumseh had an American friend, Captain Lecroix, who fought against the British and was taken prisoner. Hearing that Lecroix was sent to Montreal, Tecumseh forced Proctor to ask for Lecroix's release. Proctor had very few successes in battles, and they all were thanks to Tecumseh. He promptly issued an order that said: "The King of the Woods desires the release of Captain Lecroix, who must be set at liberty without delay."

Soon Americans started winning. General Procter kept evading battles and Tecumseh's native allies were deserting. Tecumseh is quoted pleading with Proctor to fight: "Our lives are in the hands of the Great Spirit. We are determined to defend our lands, and if it is his will, we will leave our bones here...We will stand here and give battle. My warriors and I were not made for running away from the enemies." Tecumseh knew that he had become a living legend, a symbol of the native people's fight against the injustices of colonization. Even Americans who were fighting against him openly admired him for his courage, loyalty, and noble character.

Finally, Tecumseh and Procter faced the Americans at the Battle of the Thames. Before the battle Tecumseh addressed his warriors: "Brother warriors, I shall never come out of this battle alive. I know I am going to die, but I go. My body will remain on the field, I know it will be so." He unbuckled his sword, and handed it to one of his Chiefs. "When my son becomes a great warrior, give him this sword, and tell him his father died like a brave chief and a hero. Tell my people I died for their rights." He also took off the British uniform, and put on his Indian deerskin hunting clothes and war-paint. Tecumseh perished in fighting. General Procter fled from the battlefield.

"The last of their race" by John Mix Stanley

OSCEOLA
1804 – 1838

The Indian leader Osceola was born in Alabama. His heritage was both Native American and European. His mother was a mixed-race native-white woman raised in a Creek (Muscogee) tribe. One of her grandfathers was a Scottish settler, James McQueen. Osceola's uncle, Peter McQueen was one of the leaders of the Red Stick rebellion – an attempt to force white settlers off of Creek lands. After the Muscogee Creeks were defeated by United States forces in 1814, Osceola's family moved to Spanish Florida and was adopted by the Seminole people – an alliance of various Native American tribes that migrated to Florida in the 18th century.

Portrait of Osceola by George Catlin, 1838

THE TRAIL OF TEARS

The Trail of Tears was the forced relocation of around 60,000 American Indians from their ancestral lands in the southeastern US to the "Indian Territory" west of the Mississippi River, between 1830 and 1850. The relocated people included the Cherokee, Muscogee (Creek), Seminole, Chickasaw, and Choctaw nations. Some tribes purchased captive Africans and kept them as slaves. As a result, thousands of black slaves accompanied their owners on The Trail of Tears.

In 1821 Florida was purchased from Spain by the United States. Seminole Indians were offered money for their land if they moved West, but the Seminole chiefs replied, "This is the land of our forefathers. Spaniards never bought it from us, and they cannot sell it to you. We do not recognize your right, and we shall not move." Before the Florida purchase, the Spanish offered shelter to black slaves who escaped from the United States. The Spanish even offered slaves free land in Florida. The Seminoles, too, rejected slavery, so many escaped slaves stayed with the Seminoles and married into their tribes.

When Osceola became one of the tribal chiefs, he took two wives, according to the custom of his people. Legends say that one of them was black, the daughter of an escaped slave, and that when Osceola and his wife were visiting one of the United States forts, she was seized and claimed as a slave by her mother's former master. Even though there are no historical sources to prove this story, it clearly reflects the fact the Seminoles were against slavery. This legend is also often quoted to explain why Osceola didn't hesitate to call the Seminoles to war.

But the bitter history itself – tribe after tribe being ousted from their lands – was probably enough to convince a proud native leader to organize resistance.

In 1832, a few Seminole chiefs met with the US Indian agent, General Wiley Thompson. They were supposed to sign the Treaty of Payne's Landing in which they agreed to leave their Florida lands in exchange for lands west of the Mississippi River. The treaty gave the Seminoles three years to move away. Osceola was present, and listened in silence to the talk of both parties. When they called on him to sign the treaty, he drew his knife, and struck it deep into the paper before him. "With that knife, and with that alone, will I negotiate with the white man for the lands of my forefathers," he said, and walked out.

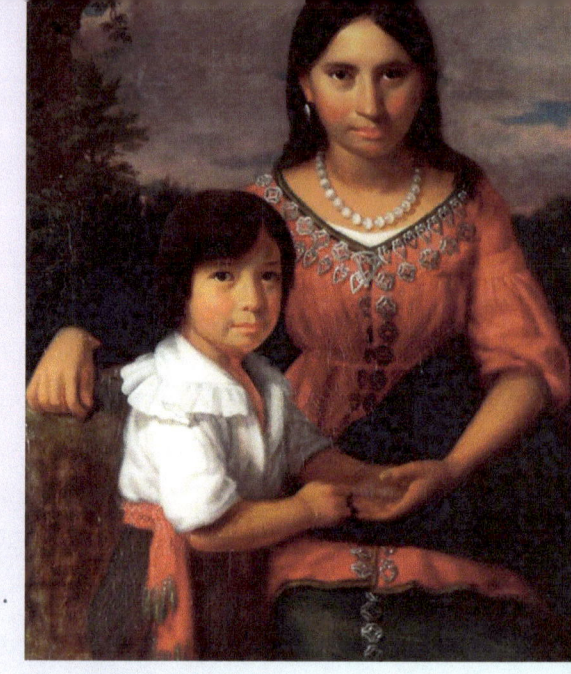

The 'Sedgeford Hall Portrait', possibly depicting Osceola's wife and son

When five Seminole chiefs sided with Osceola, Thompson declared that those chiefs who did notsign the treaty were not to be considered tribal leaders anymore. Then he reported to the government, "The Indians, after they had received the annuity (payments for the land sold to the US government), purchased an unusually large quantity of gunpowder and lead. Fearing a rebellion, Thompson prohibited the sale of guns and ammunition to the Seminoles. Osceola took this as an insult – the Seminoles were being treated like slaves (who were not allowed to own weapons). "The white man shall not make me black," he told his chiefs. "I will make the white man red with blood; and then blacken him in the sun and rain... and the buzzards will feed upon his flesh."

"The Seminole War in the Everglades"; Left: Seminole girls in Florida, 1948

In the summer of 1835 a group of white farmers looking for lost cattle, seized some Seminole tribesmen, who, they claimed, had stolen and cooked their cows. The farmers disarmed the tribesmen and tried to whip them. But more Seminole men arrived and opened fire on the farmers. A few people were wounded in the fight. Two months later a US soldier carrying the mail from Fort Brooke to Fort King was ambushed and killed by Seminole warriors.

The Seminoles were now on the path of war. They started attacking remote farms, stage coaches, and army forts. They even burned the Cape Florida lighthouse. Word was sent by Osceola to all Seminole tribes that any chief who signed any treaty with the whites, or who agreed to go West should be put to death. In the fall Chief Charley Emathla, fearing a war, decided to move his people out of Florida and sold his cattle at Fort King. Osceola ambushed Emathla on his way back to his village, killed him, and scattered the money from the cattle sale across the dead body.

Despite the tensions, Osceola kept communicating with General Thompson, who kept pressure on the Seminoles to sign the Treaty of Payne's Landing. Osceola knew Thompson very well. He often came to his office to report about the wrongs committed by white settlers against the Seminole tribespeople. Thompson even considered Osceola a friend, and had given him a rifle as a gift. In the fall of 1835 after an argument about the treaty, Thompson ordered Osceola arrested and locked him up at Fort King for two nights. Osceola had to buy his release by signing the hated Treaty of Payne's Landing. He didn't forgive this humiliation and secretly gathered his warriors for an attack on Thompson.

"The border lands" by Edgar Samuel Paxson

On December 28, 1835, Osceola and his warriors burst into a house near Fort King where General Thomson was having dinner with his friends. With the rifle Thompson gave him, Osceola shot Thomson dead, and then scalped him. Six more guests were also shot. Next Osceola's band attacked a unit of the US Army being sent from Fort Brooke to Fort King. 140 soldiers were ambushed. All were killed. Not even the wounded were spared. Following their ancient tradition, the tribesmen collected scalps. This event became known as the Dade Massacre.

Seminole tribes had their homes along the edges of the swamps, and deep in the Everglades of Florida. These pathless regions were almost inaccessible to the US soldiers sent to fight the rebels. All across Florida, settlers were terrified. Whole towns were abandoned, as settlers fled to the forts for protection. In 1836, Seminole warriors and their black allies attacked 21 plantations and won the Battle of Wahoo Swamp against a US army force numbering 2500 soldiers. But not all local native tribes were on the side of the Seminoles. Their old enemies, the Creek, sided with the US army. A volunteer Creek cavalry unit that fought against the Seminoles was led by the first Native American graduate of the U.S. Military Academy at West Point, David Moniac, who was of mixed, native-Scottish heritage. David Moniac perished in the Battle of Wahoo Swamp.

By the end of 1836, the US army commander in Florida, Thomas Jesup, raised an army of over 9000 men to fight the Seminole rebellion. Half of his army were volunteers – white settlers and members of native tribes hostile to the Seminoles.

'Early dawn attack' by Charles Schreyvogel

Under Jesup, the US army started winning. In January 1837 some Seminole chiefs signed a "Capitulation" document and surrendered.

To save the black allies of the Seminoles from slavery, they were included in the agreement as the 'property' of the Seminole tribes, and were allowed to follow their 'owners' in their removal to the West. The Seminole and black warriors who surrendered were kept in a holding camp at Fort Brooke. Osceola and his fighters attacked the camp and liberated 700 fighters. In response Thomas Jesup ordered that Osceola be seized and thrown into prison when he came to the fort to negotiate under a white flag of truce.

The American public was outraged by Jesup's betrayal of the truce rules. It was declared to be "one of the most disgraceful acts in American military history." Nevertheless, Osceola and other captives remained in prison. Osceola suffered from chronic malaria. In prison his condition worsened and three months after his capture he died. During his captivity he was visited by friends and three artists – George Catlin, W. M. Laning, and Robert John Curtis, who each painted a portrait of Osceola.

"Osceola of Florida" by Robert John Curtis
Right: the "Treaty of Fort Gibson"

Sitting Bull
1831 – 1890

The Indian chief Sitting Bull became famous for unifying and leading the Sioux native tribes in their resistance to the policies of the US government. However, his first battle against the American Army occurred when he was already over 30 years old, and a seasoned warrior. Until then he was heavily involved in inter-tribal wars for trails and hunting lands – the bitter hostilities between native tribes that were readily used by the American government to weaken and defeat the Indians of the Great Plains.

Sitting Bull was born in the Lakota tribe in what would later become the Dakota Territory. His birth name was Jumping Badger. When he was growing up, ambushing and killing Crow Indians – the enemies of the Lakota – was almost a sport among the kids of his tribe. It was done to develop the warrior qualities in young men. Sitting Bull first ambushed and shot a Crow warrior traveling alone on a trail claimed by the Lakota, and then he shot and killed a whole family – mother, father, and a baby. At age 14, he joined the warriors of his tribe in a raid to seize horses from a Crow camp. Bravery in that raid earned him his grown-up name – Four Horns. From his father, Jumping Bull, received an eagle feather, a horse, and a buffalo skin shield – the symbols of a warrior. Later his father perished in combat with Crow Indians, and Sitting Bull took another name – "Buffalo Who Sits Down."

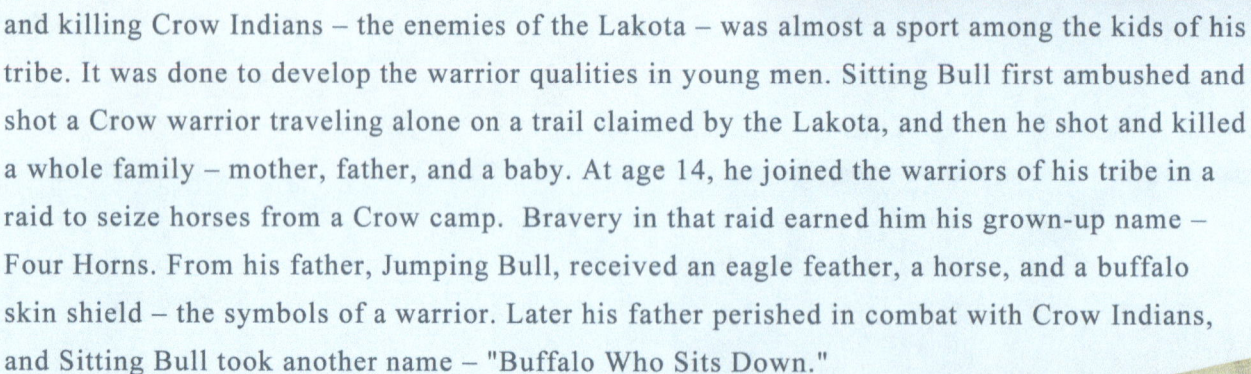

Sitting Bull liked to have his victories over his enemies recorded in drawings. Some of these pictures, drawn on the pages of a military roster book by an unknown artist, can be seen in the American Museum of Natural History. They show native warriors, white men – armed and unarmed – and women, all shot dead by Sitting Bull, with his name signed on every page.

This enthusiasm for war and warrior culture earned Sitting Bull the reputation of being a cruel and relentless enemy. He was dreaded, even as a young man. One of his biographers wrote about him, "He possesses much force of mind, with a genius for war, and a stubborn heroism, admirable in the champion of a race."

COUP COUNTING

The word 'coup' means 'a blow' in French. 'Coup counting' is the name given by Europeans to a custom of counting acts of bravery in battles practiced by the Plains Indians, including the Lakota. Native people had a point system for various acts of bravery. The highest points were given for touching a live enemy in combat with a hand or with a special coup stick – and escaping unharmed. The enemy didn't have to be killed – touching him was supposed to humiliate him. Coups were recorded by notches on the coup stick. The award for a coup was permission to wear certain colors of war paint and feathers.

Cheyenne warrior touches his Crow enemy with a coup stick

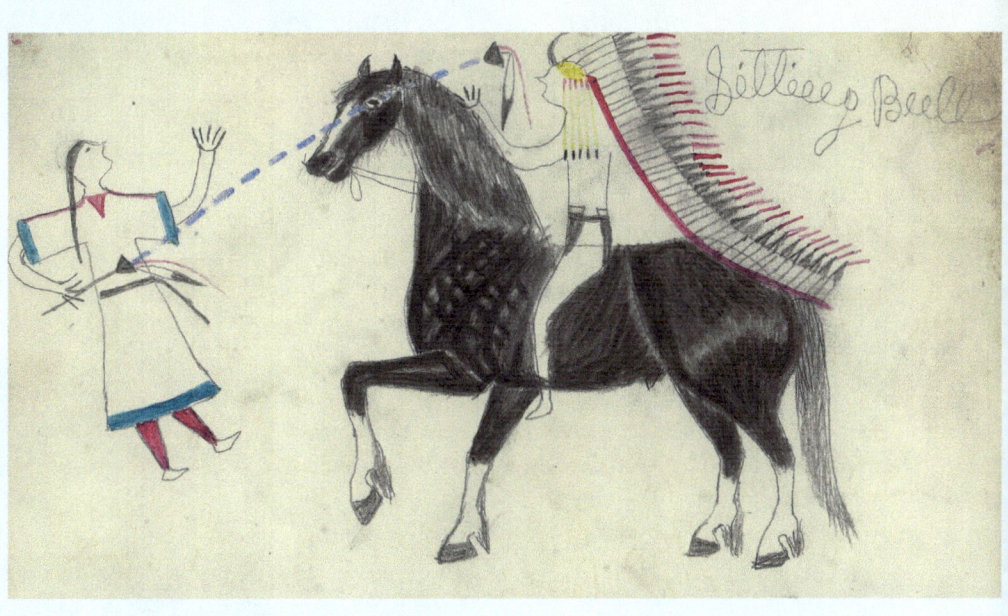

In 1862, as the Civil War was raging, the US Government failed to keep its promises to protect the hunting grounds of the Eastern Dakota Indians.

In response, native bands killed about 800 white settlers who moved onto their land. Sitting Bull's tribe didn't participate in these raids ('the Dakota War') but the following year the US Army arrived to suppress the uprising, and attacked all local tribes, whether they had been involved in the raids against the settlers or not. Sitting Bull called together Lakota warriors to defend his people. They stood no chance, however, against over 2000 US soldiers. The Lakota and Dakota were defeated and driven out of their lands.

In 1866, another Lakota leader, Red Cloud, led his warriors to besiege a few US Army forts in Montana. Sitting Bull joined Red Cloud in this uprising, which became known as the 'Red Cloud's War,' but two years later Red Cloud signed a peace treaty with the US, and the tribes he represented moved to the newly-created Great Sioux Reservation. Many Sioux tribes agreed to move because overhunting had caused their buffalo herds to grow smaller and smaller. Lacking meat, more and more Sioux bands chose to sell their lands to the government for a trickle of payments that would at least guarantee their survival.

Red Cloud

Sitting Bull felt betrayed. He rejected Red Cloud's treaty and continued to attack US army forts and settlers' wagon trains. In the 1870s his band drove away the surveyors sent to explore the Lakota and Dakota territories to decide where to build the Northern Pacific Railway. The railway engineers returned twice accompanied by US troops, but again and again, Sitting Bull wouldn't let them work.

'Buffalo Hunt' by John Mix Stanley

BUFFALO

For the native tribes of The Great Plains, the buffalo, or bison, was the main source of food, clothes, and materials for tools. Up to the middle of the 19th century, millions of bison roamed the North American plains. For thousands of years native people hunted buffalo on foot, with spear and bow-and-arrow. But when the European colonists arrived with horses and firearms, the hunting of buffalo became much more efficient. Too efficient. In the 19th century, white and native hunters killed over 50 million buffalo. The numbers of buffalo dropped, and the native tribes who relied on buffalo for survival became dependent on the colonists for supplies, including the guns and gunpowder now needed for hunting.

'Buffalo Chase' by Alfred Jacob Miller

"Medicine Man" by Charles M. Russel

Meanwhile, in the Black Hills of South Dakota, they discovered gold. The Dakota refused to sell the Black Hills to the US government, so the government started looking for a way to get out of the treaty signed by Red Cloud and seize the Sioux land. President Grant ordered all Sioux bands to move to the Great Sioux Reservation – this time whether they wanted to or not. Anyone who stayed 'off the reservation' would be removed by force. Grant knew that Sitting Bull would never agree to live on a reservation, and that this refusal would make him the leader of a 'hostile' band and an official enemy of the US.

Grant was right. Sitting Bull began preparing for another war. He brought together 10,000 warriors and their families from 10 Sioux bands and the Northern Cheyenne tribes, and formed a band he named "Strong Hearts." The Strong Hearts camped in Montana, in a remote area called "the Badlands."

They were well-armed, because the US government had supplied the Lakota with the best arms and ammunition in accordance with the treaty signed by Red Cloud. At that point Sitting Bull considered himself the spiritual leader of his movement – more a medicine-man than a warrior. He organized a Sun Dance – a traditional gathering with dances, songs, fasting, and various rituals that tested the strength and endurance of warriors. The US and Canadian governments viewed sun dances as a form of preparation for war, so later they were banned.

At the Sun Dance, Sitting Bull told his followers that a powerful spirit talked to him and gave him knowledge and orders. He said he had had a vision: 'The Great Spirit has given our enemies to us. We are to destroy them.' Convinced that the uprising was inevitable, the US government sent troops under the command of Lt. Colonel George Armstrong Custer. Colonel Custer approached Sitting Bull's camp and attacked. Sioux forces, led by Sitting Bull's ally, Crazy Horse, pushed back against Custer's troops and drove them to the cliffs above the Little Bighorn River. The American force was wiped out. Even Colonel Custer himself was killed.

'Custer's Last Stand' by Edgar Samuel Paxson

The following year the US government struck back, sending thousands of troops. Most Sioux bands surrendered. There was a split in the camp of Sitting Bull. Some of his chiefs accused him of cowardice, saying that during the Battle of the Little Bighorn he took his family and left to sit out the battle in a safe place far away. They said that he was in such a hurry that he abandoned one of his small twin kids in a tent by the Little Bighorn River. To humiliate Sitting Bull, they named the twins "The One Taken" and "The One Left."

The very idea of the war against the government was becoming less and less popular. Many younger Lakota didn't mind living on a reservation, getting education, and becoming part of American society. Feeling betrayed and bitter, Sitting Bull and his followers refused to surrender and crossed the border into Canada.
For about five years, Sitting Bull lived in the Canadian Northwest. But feeding his people became a challenge – again, because of the rapidly decreasing buffalo population. In 1881 Sitting Bull was approached by the Americans offering him pardon if he surrendered. Sitting Bull's response was: "If you have one honest man in Washington, send him here, and I'll talk to him." Nevertheless, after many hardships, Sitting Bull and his people surrendered to the US government.

At the surrender Sitting Bull stated, "I wish it to be remembered that I was the last man of my tribe to surrender my rifle." Until 1883 Sitting Bull and his family were held prisoners of war in a fort in the Dakota Territory. Then they were released on parole. Sitting Bull at last went to live on the reservation. Civil War General Oliver Howard, who served at the office of Indian Affairs and knew Sitting Bull well, wrote about Sitting Bull's life after the Great Sioux War: "Sitting Bull was a born diplomat, a ready speaker, and in middle life he ceased to go on the warpath, to become an advisor to his people."

In 1884, a businessman and show promoter, Alvaren Allen from Minnesota, came up with the idea of an open-air show that would feature Native American customs, skills, stories and personalities. Sitting Bull, along with a few of his friends and their wives, agreed to become the stars of his show – "The Sitting Bull Combination." The show went touring from town to town. As part of the show, Sitting Bull made a speech talking about the needs of his people for education and financial help. The interpreter, however, always translated his speech into English with a pre-written script where Sitting Bull supposedly told the story of killing General Custer. Soon the government authorities learned that a fake story of Custer's death was featured in the show, and the show was canceled.

Almost immediately, however, Sitting Bull and 20 of his warriors received an invitation to join another show – the famous "Buffalo Bill's Wild West," organized by the US showman William Cody who got the nickname "Buffalo Bill" when he worked as a buffalo hunter to supply railroad workers with meat. The show included a cowboys-and-Indians parade, horse races, music, a demonstration of cowboy and native skills and crafts, and more. Show performers also reenacted Indian attacks on wagon trains, stagecoach robberies, and told the story of the Pony Express. At "Buffalo Bill's Wild West" shows, Sitting Bull sat in a tent on the showgrounds selling Indian crafts – beaded bags, bow-and-arrow sets. His contract with the promoters of the show included the following line: "Sitting Bull is to have sole rights to sell his own photographs and autographs." The show made Sitting Bull famous in the US and abroad, and soon he was making good money selling his autographs. Sitting Bull came home carrying hundreds of dollars, which he gave to his people.

A reporter for the Buffalo, New York, newspaper *The Courier* met Sitting Bull and wrote about him: "He had no wish for blood in his heart. He was sorry the white man was not as honest as he was full of brain power... He hoped that the red man had enough self-respect and the white man enough honesty left to make the end of the controversy a peaceful one."

Sitting Bull and Buffalo Bill;
Left: 'Buffalo Bill fighting the Indians' by Louis Maurer

During his time touring with the shows, Sitting Bull met the famous sharpshooter and instructor of women's self-defense Annie Oakley. Sitting Bull was impressed with her skill. She could shoot with either hand – with inhuman accuracy. One of her acts was shooting out a cigar from her husband's lips from a significant distance. After Buffalo Bill himself, Annie was the highest-paid performer in the show. Sitting Bull offered money to have his photograph taken with Annie, and later symbolically adopted Oakley as his daughter, naming her "Little Sure Shot." In her turn, Annie Oakley admired Sitting Bull, and used her Lakota name throughout her career.

In 1889 a new spiritual movement was born among the Nevada native tribes – the Ghost Dance movement. It invited native people to dance and chant in order to wake up their ancestors who would rise from the dead and drive the white Americans from the Indian lands. Dancers – men and women together – held hands and moved slowly around in a circle, wearing shirts that were said to stop bullets. The Ghost Dance movement spread like wildfire all across the American West, causing the US government to fear a massive Indian uprising might lie ahead. Sitting Bull never gave up the hope of unifying the tribes against the white settlers, so he allowed the Ghost Dance ceremony to be performed at his camp on the Grand River. That made him a target.

Annie Oakley

The government sent troops to camp near Sitting Bull's reservation. Many native people started leaving for the Badlands, fearing war. It looked like Sitting Bull might join them and become one of the leaders of the Ghost Dance movement. To prevent this, the Indian agency police were sent to Sitting Bull's house to arrest him.

Lakota Ghost Dance shirt.

When Sitting Bull refused to leave his house, the police tried to seize him. Lakota warriors heard the noise from Sitting Bull's house and rushed there. One of them opened fire on the police. In response, two native policemen, Bull Head and Red Tomahawk, shot and killed Sitting Bull.

In 1915 Red Tomahawk gave an interview in which he said: "I was a Sergeant of the Indian Police. Sitting Bull was my friend. I killed him like this... I grabbed his left arm and I had my gun in my hand, too. I told him not to call his people or we would kill him. But when we got outside, he made a loud cry when he saw his son come from around the corner. Then the hostiles (Sitting Bull's followers) came. His son, Crow Foot, was killed right away. I shot Sitting Bull in the left side. He fell face down. I shot him again in the back of the neck. He was dead then."

The interviewer asked Red Tomahawk "Does Sitting Bull's spirit ever come back here?"
"Yes, sometimes," answered Red Tomahawk. "He rides in on an elk."
"I want to go to his grave," said the interviewer. "Come with me."
"No. I am afraid," responded Red Tomahawk. "There are mysterious flowers on his grave every year. We don't know where they come from. They are Wankan."

'Wankan' means 'the Great Spirit' in Lakota.

Right: Sitting Bull and his family in 1881:
left to right – Sitting Bull's mother, his sister,
Sitting Bull, his two daughters and a grandson;
below: Sioux village, 1879

Chief Joseph
1840 – 1904

Chief Joseph's native name translated as "Thunder Rolling Down the Abyss." He was born to Joseph, the chief of the Nez Percé tribe, which was one of the most powerful tribes of the Pacific Northwest. The native name of this tribe is Nimíipuu which means 'the people.' Nez Percé – 'a pierced nose' in French – is a nickname given to the Nez Percé by French fur traders. The Nez Percé welcomed white settlers, and many of them converted to Christianity, including Chief Joseph's father. Chief Joseph was baptized as well, and went to a Christian mission school.

In 1855 Chief Joseph's father, along with other Nez Percé chiefs, signed the Treaty of Walla Walla with the United States. The treaty stated that most of the Nez Percé ancestral lands would form a reservation stretching across present-day Idaho, Oregon, and Washington. But then gold was discovered in Oregon, and in 1863 the US government asked the Nez Percé to sell more land and move to the Idaho portion of the reservation in exchange for payments, schools, and a hospital. Again, many Nez Percé chiefs agreed, but Chief Joseph's father, whose land in the Wallowa Valley, Oregon, was to be sold, refused to sign the new treaty.

In 1871, on his deathbed, Chief Joseph's father told him: "Always remember that your father never sold his country. You must stop your ears whenever you are asked to sign a treaty selling your home. A few years more and white men will be all around you. They have their eyes on this land. My son, never forget my dying words. This country holds your father's body. Never sell the bones of your father and your mother."

After his father died, Chief Joseph became the chief of the Wallowa band of Nez Percé. Despite the continuing pressure of the government, he did everything to preserve peace. When US prospectors – geologists looking for possible gold-mining sites – showed up on the Nez Percé land, Chief Joseph prevented his people from attacking them. But some clashes did occur – the native warriors killed a few white newcomers who tried to settle in the Wallowa Valley. White settlers pushed back and native blood was shed as well. As a result, in 1877 the government sent General Oliver O. Howard to force the Wallowa band to relocate to Idaho.

Years later Howard wrote a book "Famous Indian Chiefs I have Known" where he told the story of Chief Joseph. When they met, Howard asked Chief Joseph to go together and look at the lands the government offered to the Nez Percé. "We rode over forty miles together," wrote Howard, "and Joseph said to me: 'If we come and live here, what will you give us – schools, teachers, houses, churches, and gardens?' I said, 'Yes.' 'Well,' said Joseph, 'those are just the things we don't want. The Earth is our mother, and do you think we want to dig and break it? No! We want to hunt buffalo and fish for salmon, not plow the land.'"

The land that General Howard showed to Chief Joseph was inhabited by both white settlers and native people. "We would clear out all these people," promised Howard. But in the Nez Percé tradition, taking the land that did not belong to them was prohibited. Howard, however, didn't want to hear any objections. He gave the Nez Percé 30 days to move to the reservation. Chief Joseph took a hard decision – the Nez Percé would move to Idaho.

Many chiefs disagreed with him and demanded to go on the warpath. But Joseph felt peace was more important than living on the ancestral land. As the Nez Percé were preparing for the move, the land-grabbing settlers were impatient, and did everything they could to provoke the Indians to violence in order to speed up their eviction. Soon Chief Joseph heard that three young Nez Percé warriors had killed a group of white settlers to avenge the murder of a family member. "Down with the bloodthirsty savages!" was the cry of the outraged settlers.

Chief Joseph and his family, 1880

"Now began all sorts of trouble," wrote General Howard. "The Indians stole horses, burned houses, robbed travelers, and the whole country was wild with terror. Joseph at first did not know what to do, but at last he broke his agreement with me and went on the warpath." Actually, Chief Joseph was, again, trying to avoid war. He had only between 200 and 300 warriors. Howard's troops outnumbered the Nez Percé warriors 10 to 1. Together with their families, the Wallowa band was about 750 people.

As General Howard's troops were approaching, ready for battle, Chief Joseph thought of the potential loss of life and decided to take his people to Montana, where he was planning to ask the Crow Nation in the Montana Territory for refuge. But the Crow refused to help the Nez Percé. Then Chief Joseph led his band north hoping to join Sitting Bull's Lakota band. The 3-month-long retreat of the Nez Percé pursued by Oliver Howard's troops across Oregon, Washington, Idaho, and Montana, became known as the Nez Percé War.

Chief Joseph was a good military leader. On a few occasions his small band managed to defeat the American troops through spectacular maneuvers. All the American newspapers were reporting about the Nez Percé War and Chief Joseph became a celebrity. His fame was due not only to his successes in battles, but also to the fact that he never killed prisoners, women, children, or the elderly, and purchased food from local farmers and storekeepers rather than robbing them.

The famous General Sherman of the Union Army wrote about the Nez Percé War: "Throughout this extraordinary campaign the Indians displayed courage and skill that everybody praised. They didn't scalp the dead, let captive women go free, did not murder indiscriminately, and fought with scientific skill, using advance and rear guards, skirmish lines, and field fortifications." By the way, General Sherman's full name was William Tecumseh Sherman, because his father was a fan of the great chief of the Shawnee, Tecumseh.

'Surrender of Chief Joseph'
by Edgar Samuel Paxton

"For many months there were battles – battles – battles!" wrote General Howard. "Joseph was a splendid warrior, and with many of Uncle Sam's good soldiers he fought. I followed him for over 1400 miles, over mountains and valleys, always trying to make him give up. At last I sent two Nez Percé friends, Captain John and Indian George to Chief Joseph's stronghold in the Little Rockies with a white flag to ask him to give up. Joseph responded: 'I have done all I can. I now trust my people and myself to your mercy.'"

"So the surrender was arranged, and just before night on October 5, 1877, Joseph, followed by his people, many of whom were wounded, came to me and offered his rifle. Beside me stood General N. A. Miles, who had helped me and fought the last battle, and so I told Joseph that General Miles would accept the rifle for me."

The newspapers published Chief Joseph's speech at the surrender. Even though scholars debate whether Joseph actually made this speech, it became famous: "I am tired of fighting. Our chiefs are killed... It is cold, and we have no blankets. Our little children are freezing to death. My people, some of them, have run away to the hills, and have no blankets, no food. No one knows where they are – perhaps freezing to death. I want to have time to look for my children, to see how many I can find. Maybe I shall find them among the dead. Hear me, my chiefs! I am tired. My heart is sick and sad. From where the sun now stands, I will fight no more forever."

By the end of the war 150 of Chief Joseph's warriors were dead. The remaining warriors and their families were sent to a prisoners-of-war camp, and after a few months to the Indian Territory in Oklahoma. That was a violation of the terms of the Nez Percé surrender, which promised the Wallowa band a chance to return to the Wallowa Valley in Oregon. Almost a third of the Nez Percé died along the way from hardships and diseases. Chief Joseph went to Washington, D.C. twice asking first President Rutherford Hayes and then President Theodore Roosevelt to allow his people to return to Idaho. But the government in Idaho did everything to prevent his return. In 1897 Chief Joseph rode with Buffalo Bill in a parade in New York City, but no amount of celebrity helped him to return his people to the Pacific Northwest. Finally, the remaining Wallowa band was allowed to move to the Colville Indian Reservation in Nespelem, Washington, still far from the rest of the Nez Percé and from the Wallowa Valley.

Piegan native village, 1900

In his late years Chief Joseph realized that to stand their ground in America his people needed education. He became an advocate for the education of the native tribes, insisting that all Indian kids should go to school.

"27 years later," wrote General Howard in his book, "I came to see Chief Joseph, the greatest Indian warrior I ever fought, at the Carlisle Indian School, and there, in a speech, he said: 'For a long time I wanted to kill General Howard, but now I am glad to see him, and we are friends.'"

General Howard and Chief Josesph had this photo taken at the Carlisle Indian School.

Vintage photos from the 1900s

Naavajo young man

*Above: Chief Wolf Robe, Cheyenne;
Below: Navajo medicine man*